Classical modern architecture

Classical modern architecture

ANDREAS PAPADAKIS

·TERRAIL·

Front cover
Allan Greenberg
Huckleberry House
Connecticut, USA

Frontispiece
Allan Greenberg
Huckleberry House, Porch
Connecticut, USA

Editors: Jean-Claude Dubost and Jean-François Gonthier
Art Director: Bruno Leprince
Cover design: Gérard Lo Monaco and Laurent Gudin
Typesetting : Graffic, Paris
Lithography: Litho Service T. Zamboni, Verona

© FINEST S.A. / EDITIONS PIERRE TERRAIL, PARIS 1997
© English edition, 1997
An imprint of the book department
of Bayard Presse S.A.
ISBN: 2-87939-119-9
Printed in Italy

CONTENTS

THE CLASSICAL TRADITION

ANDREAS PAPADAKIS

"I believe that when a man loses contact with the past he loses his soul. Likewise, if we deny the architectural past – and the lessons to be learned from our ancestors – then our buildings also lose their souls. If we abandon the traditional principles upon which architecture was based for 2,500 years or more, then our civilization suffers." HRH the Prince of Wales

"The classical is that which speaks of tradition in a modern voice thus highlighting man's capacity for millennial continuity. The classical reaches across culture and time and, taking the risk of anachronism, it heals the estrangement which humanism constantly faces. The classical, then, is certainly the enduring and the timeless. But this timelessness always takes the form of modernity; that is, it takes the form of the relevance of tradition." Demetri Porphyrios

Opposite

Porphyrios Associates
Magdalen College
Oxford, United Kingdom
New Longwall Quadrangle, detail

My aim in compiling this book is to show the best of Modern Classical Architecture in all its richness and variety by presenting the work not only of leading international architects but also projects by younger architects experimenting with classical architecture today. Classical buildings are both memorable and familiar because of their human proportions and human scale. From time immemorial classical architecture has had a rich repertoire further enhanced by neo-classical revivals reflecting the spirit of their time.

At the beginning of the twentieth century it became clear that a new, simpler architecture was needed to reflect the growing populations and expanding cities of the industrial age. A spontaneous response occurred in many countries: in France, Auguste Perret's building without orders and ornamentation was predictably dubbed 'stripped-down' classicism by the critics; and at the

same time, in Germany, Tessenow and his students developed their own classical style. In affluent Sweden, where a significant neo-classical movement developed, even low cost housing was classical in its simplest form. But in Germany the rise of the modern movement promoted a new spirit of industrialization in a nation impatient with slowly-evolving ways. This, and the of two world wars and their aftermath, led to the spread of a more regimented architecture judged by the number of built units rather than beauty or appropriateness, with unfortunate results.

However, for more than a decade now there has been a strong reaction against such soulless architecture and cities. A small group of pioneers, led by Leon Krier and subsequently helped by the patronage and support of the Prince of Wales, has succeeded in re-establishing continuity with the past. Leon Krier has formulated, in simple, precise language accessible to students, architects and the public alike, a series of propositions that explain the strengths of Modern Classicism, stressing both its appropriateness to today and the intricate relationship between the vernacular and the classical.

Distinguished architects have helped to consolidate these gains. Allan Greenberg in America uses a language appropriate to significant public buildings such as the Treaty Suite at the Department of State in Washington and private houses, showing that gracious living is not restricted to buildings of the past. Other American architects, including Jaquelin Robertson, have been influenced by American neo-classicism.

In Britain, Quinlan Terry surprised architects and developers alike with his successful and controversial Richmond Riverside office development, where he rejected a brief for an office block in favour of a series of low-rise spaces. Robert Adam has responded to a more austere language related to English Palladian prototypes, while Demetri Porphyrios and his thriving international practice have contributed a number of highly influential didactic pavilions as well as a substantial body of built work ranging from a more relaxed classical vernacular to formal civic buildings.

Debate about the reconstruction of the European city has focused on the rue de Laeken in Brussels. Other projects approaching fruition include the proposal for Paternoster Square in the City of London, which would be the largest classical ensemble to date. It is perhaps in urban planning that the classical tradition has most to contribute.

Rob Krier
Ritterstrasse
Berlin, Germany

Opposite

Leon Krier
Atlantis
Watercolour by Rita Wolff

ON MODERN CLASSICAL ARCHITECTURE

BY JAMES STEELE

The historical background

The Classical period in Greece reached its apogee in a remarkably short time with the construction of the Parthenon, which was completed in 432 BC. The architectural system that coalesced in it had achieved perfection. Today there is a consensus that this perfection was the culmination of diverse cultural forces – indigenous and external – which are difficult to identify.

The Doric and Ionic orders are the primary evidence of this mix. Doric is conventionally traced to an invasion from the north by a martial strain whose harsh simplicity is recorded in the straightforward column profile that bears their name. Athens traces its origins to Ionia and the epic colonial movements across the Aegean. The wave-like volutes of the Ionic capital record its maritime origins, which are extremely ancient.

Pericles was aware of these cultural associations and the symbolic power of the orders that represented them. Indeed classical architecture did not emerge in a vacuum and was not used for purely aesthetic reasons. It had social implications that conveyed powerful sectarian messages. The Parthenon is generally portrayed as the Apollonian opposite of the Dionysian agora below, as a counterpoint to commercial transaction. It was a political manifesto in marble to rally the far-flung parts of a new Athenian Empire, the physical embodiment of the citizens' image of themselves, and a mirror of their aspirations; recorded in the frieze of the temple, the citizens' history was transformed into myth.

The perfect unity of the classical hierarchy stems from its vernacular origins. The origins of both Mycenean palace and Greek temple lie in a domestic model in wood.

Roman deviation from the classical canon, exaggerating Hellenistic licence, also had an ideological basis: mass scale and proportion were altered

Craftsman at work
*Carving of acroteria for the
Maitland Robinson Library*
Cambridge, United Kingdom

Opposite
Quinlan Terry
**Maitland Robinson Library,
Downing College**
Cambridge, United Kingdom

to create the image that the new republic wanted to project as an emerging power on the ancient world stage. While Greek models were at first followed fairly closely, the Republic adopted the familiar historical tactic of attempting to establish legitimacy through formal appropriation that included Etruscan precedents.

During the Renaissance, Roman paradigms prevailed, and architects freely interpreted the ancient models that they measured. Brunelleschi was one of the first to begin this loose adaptation, in buildings such as the Pazzi chapel, where Corinthian columns were used in the porch and in the pilasters of the interior. It reached its zenith in Michelangelo's "monumental order" on the Campidoglio. But Palladio's Basilica in Vicenza and the nearby Villa Rotonda were more influential in subsequent European revivals.

During the eighteenth century there was a renewed interest in classical architecture. Three surveys of Selinus, Paestum and Agrigentum were published between 1726 and 1746. A detailed study of the Parthenon itself, by the French archaeologist Leroy, appeared five years after Laugier's *Essai sur l'architecture*. This latter was an impassioned plea for a return to simplicity, which praised in the Primitive Hut a duplicate of the wooden, proto period Doric Greek temple. Laugier's work reflects the idealized, utopian view of the classical prevalent at this time.

Meanwhile, Renaissance interpretation of Classicism in England took a very different form, primarily due to Inigo Jones and Christopher Wren. Jones had travelled to Rome to study stage design, and was profoundly affected by Renaissance architecture, particularly the Palladian variant. There had been earlier attempts in Britain to follow the Italian lead, mainly in manor houses, but Inigo Jones brought his own version of Classicism into the public realm with his design for the Banqueting House in Whitehall Palace, London (1619), the church of St. Paul, Covent Garden, for the Earl of Bedford (1636) and the Queen's House in Greenwich (1635). The new aesthetic awareness enhanced by Jones's work was firmly established in the national consciousness by Christopher Wren, whose design for St. Paul's Cathedral (1675-1710) in the City of London made Classicism a national style.

Charles Vandenhove and Associates
Housing, square and fountain
Maastricht, Netherlands

Opposite
Top
Charles Vandenhove and Associates
Housing
The Hague, Netherlands
Bottom
John Simpson
The Market
Poundbury, United Kingdom

13

The Relevance of Classicism today

The twentieth century began in classical form with the stripped down Classicism of Auguste Perret's Théâtre des Champs Elysées in 1912, and with Tony Garnier's Cité Industrielle, which constituted the primary point of departure for Le Corbusier's early work from 1916 to 1928. Thus, the Modern Movement, widely considered averse to Classical principles, was inextricably linked with them. Le Corbusier extolled the Parthenon in *Vers une architecture*; Mies van der Rohe and other founders expressed their historical debt to Classicism. And it was the Modernist sensibility that largely established the framework by which other contemporary architecture is evaluated today.

The hermetic isolation and dislocation of modern life run against the human grain, and Classicism addresses our need to be a part of nature. Derived from timber vernacular architecture, it has retained detailed indications of its origins, in architrave, entablature, dentils, and guttae that are durable representations of hand-crafted components. More importantly, as Edmund Bacon has demonstrated, trabeation (the beam and post system) maintains a fine balance between architecture and nature, establishing a harmonious medium in which neither dominates. Trabeation joins architecture to the landscape around it: the Stoa of Attalus in Athens remains a timeless example of a classical column and beam structure providing a visual link with its surroundings. At a time when the human instinct to subdue nature seems to have been carried to its conclusion, an equally strong instinct for peace and harmony with nature has begun to emerge. Classicism speaks to this instinct, and has a more enduring and satisfying aesthetic pedigree than other, newer "ecological" alternatives.

The humanity of Classicism provides a second point of contemporary relevance. Theories of a mechanical paradise have resulted in the marginalization of the human being in favour of the "machine" (Frank Lloyd Wright's term for technology). The forces used to subdue nature eventually dehumanize those using them, and the extent of that threat is gradually being recognized. Contrary to such depersonalized initiatives, Classicism has an anthropomorphic origin, the capital, shaft and base of each of the orders being analogous to the human head, body and foot; its proportions were calculated to emphasize this equation. Pushed to the brink of theoretical and real extinction by technology, the human subject once again asserts a manifest identity.

Opposite
Helmut Peuker
Livos Building
Emern, Germany

Classicism is the architecture that has historically proclaimed this identity.

The proportions of Classical architecture relate to a sense of order, which is another point of relevance. Current interest in chaos theory has been fuelled by the realization that, even in chaos, there is order. This is not a new idea. There is a basic human yearning for order; even the most impoverished try to achieve some semblance of it in their lives. Order and nature co-exist in Classical architecture as Demetri Porphyrios says: "The Classical order sets form over the necessities of shelter and tectonics over the contingencies of construction. It provides a definitive account of the laws of nature as manifested through construction and shelter. Whereas the diversity of the contingent world is constantly on the verge of dissolution and the forms of the real world blossom and wilt, the Classical Order makes us see the inimitable laws of nature by means of tectonic fiction."

This "setting of form over the necessities of shelter" is of great importance because Classical architecture goes beyond necessity to evoke the *spirit* of shelter itself. The "primitive hut" of Abbé Laugier captured this concept precisely, marking the first urge to build, but also defining the difference between construction and architecture. Construction protects its inhabitants from the elements, keeping them warm, cool, or dry, but architecture goes beyond physical needs to address psychological *and* biological demands. Classical architecture at its best allows room for speculation, emotional comfort and dreams, which is why it can be re-invented by any architect who accepts its basic principles.

The architects presented here have successfully understood, accepted and translated those principles. Their diversity is proof of the flexibility of the classical framework, and the richness that is possible within it. Today, as the work of the architects presented here shows, Classicism is manifested in different ways.

A Classical typology

Classicism owes much to Rationalism. The reasons for this go back to the Enlightenment and the association made, in France, between the classical hierarchy and a growing desire for a systematic approach to architecture that would run parallel to a similar initiative in science. Typology emerged as the

Opposite
Tagliaventi and Associates
Zola Predosa Townhall
Bologna, Italy

classification of those things in architecture that have common features, like the categories of genus, phylum and species in biology. History became the inescapable source of form, and Classicism became the paragon, because its forms are the most durable, systematic, and recognizable. The idea of type was clarified by Quatremère de Quincy as a rule rather than a model to be copied or imitated, as guidelines rather than a precise form.

The two basic objections that have been levelled against typological procedures are that they are a vestige of an age of craft and thus have no application in a technological era; and that they are a frozen mechanism that excludes the possibility of change and emphasizes automatic repetition. But such objections ignore the differentiation between model and type. Models are indeed used in crafts to get a clear picture of the final product. But the type is liberating rather than confining, since it provides guidelines for deeper study. Architects frequently remark that constraints lead to better design, than open-ended possibilities.

The earliest sign of the regeneration of the typological approach after the decline of the Ecole des Beaux Arts appeared in the late fifties and early sixties. *The Architecture of the City* (1966) by Aldo Rossi has, in retrospect, proved to be one of the most significant works of architectural theory published in the second half of the twentieth century. Rossi defines type as "something that is permanent and complex, a logical principle that is prior to form and constitutes it." He clarifies this by saying that the type is also "a cultural element and as such can be investigated as an architectural artefact. Typology becomes in this way the analytical moment of architecture, and is readily identifiable at the level of urban artefacts."

Below
Allan Greenberg
Left: Gore Hall
University of Delaware, USA
Right: Seventh-Day Adventist Church
Burr Ridge, USA

The work of architects such as Leon Krier, who has emphasised the importance of the city, is echoed in the efforts of many young architects who, despite the small scale of their contributions, have had a significant impact on public opinion today. Since the unification of Berlin, the Reconstruction of the European City has become a pre-eminent topic in current debate.

In America "the new Urbanism," of Andres Duany and Elizabeth Plater-Zyberk has led to several new communities where the architectural language of choice is a form of Classicism; an explicit relationship is inferred between the traditional ideal of pre-industrial, or pre-vehicular America, and the architecture that evolved there in the late 18th and early 19th centuries. At Seaside, in Florida, changes in planning regulations were the first step in the making of a new order. After a long struggle with the planning authority, the project directors Duany and Plater-Zyberk, instituted ordinances on land use, allocation, lot sizes, building heights, street widths and location of parking; such relatively small, and seemingly banal details led to the regeneration of "the traditional American neighbourhood."

Significantly, the new urbanists overlap with another initiative variously called, green, eco, or sustainable architecture. Because it stresses indigenous materials, human scale, contextual concerns, a return to hand craft in some instances, and sensitivity to the environment, classical architecture meets these new preoccupations. Avant-garde architecture is now defined by this return to traditional values and models combined with environmental awareness and energy conservation, and Classicism has played a key role in addressing these concerns.

The new urbanism is not the product of a single designer, as was generally

Below
Allan Greenberg

Right: Residence
Greenwich, Connecticut, USA
Left: Tommy Hilfiger Flagship Store
Beverly Hills, USA

Roberto Pirzio Biroli
Cormor Park
Italy

Preceding pages

Quinlan Terry
The Cattle Market
Bury St. Edmunds,
United Kingdom
(Painting by Carl Laubin.)

the case in the Modernist period. The communities now emerging are ordinance or rule driven, which allows a number of like-minded architects to collaborate. This allows for a creative exchange of ideas on the development of the classical city, rather than a single, autocratic view. Judging by the public response they have received, such designs are highly successful. In contrast to the recent past, when architects sought to be as different as possible in order to draw attention to themselves, the aim today is teamwork. No longer preaching that crafts are too expensive to use, and so should not be taught, architectural schools are now teaching lost skills again, and many universities worldwide have strong departments dedicated to this goal. Progress in this regard has been painfully slow in many parts of the world, but the pace is quickening.

In addition to the urban focus of Leon and Rob Krier, Andreas Duany and Elizabeth Plater-Zyberk, Jacquelin Robertson, and Bruno Minardi, regard for context is perhaps the second most evident theme in this overview. Demetri Porphyrios has been one of the most prolific theorists of contextual aptitude. Iñiguez and Ustarroz have skilfully translated their approach to other locations, but their strong connection to their home region has been a dominating factor, whereas Porphyrios has been able to apply the essence of Classicism, the rule rather than the model, in all of his work, making it appropriate to both time and place. Others, such as François Spoerry and Charles Vandenhove, show equal skill in contextual aptitude and social or cultural commentary, but their frame of reference is again, largely regional.

A new Classicism

Another key theme relates to the historical split that occurred with the importation of the Palladian strain into Britain and the particular language that has resulted. There is controversy over the definition of "classical," with a narrow interpretation referring only to the Periclean period. A wider definition includes Roman models, and even those of the Renaissance.

The Palladian variant in Britain has also been influenced by Leon Battista Alberti, who looked at ancient ruins not only from the structural point of view, as Brunelleschi did, but with the intention of deducing the immutable rules of Classicism. His *De Re Aedificatoria*, based on the Vitruvian categorization of the orders by scale, detail, proportion and harmony, attempts to codify basic principles. However Alberti's Renaissance stress on the development of the individual and the cultivation of the will is a concept alien to Ancient Greece; it was only beginning to emerge in the Hellenistic period. In *De Re Aedificatoria*, Alberti states that the aesthetic excellence of a building depends on beauty and ornament, and he defines beauty as "the harmony and concord of all the parts achieved in such a manner that nothing can be added, taken away or altered except for the worse." In his view, beauty is innate; ornament enhances but is not integral to it.

In this regard, Robert Adam, John Simpson, Quinlan Terry and Jeremy Dixon and Edward Jones all come to mind, each of them directly influenced by the legacy of Inigo Jones and Christopher Wren. Quinlan Terry stands out in this list for the way that he has turned a national tradition to the purposes of industry and commerce, or rather restored it to them, since John Nash and the Adam brothers were also commercially minded. Regent Street, and the Royal Crescent in Bath were not designed simply to beautify their respective cities, but were property development for motivated by profit. Terry's Richmond Riverside is in the same spirit of enterprise as the masterpieces of Adam and Nash. In today's competitive economic climate, the pressures of globalization are felt throughout the industrialized world, and commercialism is necessary to ensure not only a project's success but the longevity that Classicists also seek. The focus now is just on profit, but survival. As Kenneth Powell has noted, Terry "faces the issue of imitation straight on. Like Demetri Porphyrios, he stresses that imitation has been a central feature of Western architecture for thousands of years..."

The equivalent of this tendency, again surprisingly close to historical precedent, is what might be termed American Federalism: the use of Classicism, as in traditional in the United States, to assert a democratic agenda. Allan Greenberg, Hammond Beeby and Babka, and John Blatteau are best understood in this light, although such generalizations must always be qualified. While it is tempting to mention Thomas Gordon Smith with them, he is an exception and his oeuvre raises interesting issues about the need for historical accuracy as a guiding premise. Few, apart from Leon Krier, have been as didactic in their rendition of Classicism. Their extensive scholarly research places these two architects in a category of their own, best described as Archaeological Classicism. Some architects, such as Robert Adam, claim that

Marc and Nada Breitman
New buildings
Le Plessis-Robinson, France

intention is more important than accuracy; that accuracy is impossible to achieve, since most of the relevant buildings have disappeared, and social and technological conditions have changed. Smith's work shows his determination to represent the classical spirit as closely as he can, with colour playing a vital role. The state of the surviving monuments convinced 18th century neo-classicists that ancient Greek architecture was pure white. Labrouste, in his final project at the Ecole des Beaux Arts, challenged that assumption on the basis of more accurate studies, and was almost expelled as a result. Le Corbusier's description of the Parthenon as resembling "polished steel" shows the persistence of this idea, even after Labrouste's challenge. Thomas Gordon Smith has always emphasized colour, and the wider world view that it reveals.

All the architects presented here belong to the same theoretical family, showing the diversity that is possible within the unity of Classicism. At a time when institutions are under great threat, they are participating in an attempt to halt and reverse that process, by providing stability in the face of change, and by solidifying tradition, which people in all countries, despite cultural differences, yearn for as an alternative to social chaos. Classicism has many compartments, but its underlying structure is unmistakable and urgently topical today.

Pages 24 and 25

Allan Greenberg
Beechwoods
New England, USA

Opposite

François Spoerry
Top: **Gassin,** France
Bottom: **Port Léman,** France

Overleaf

Quinlan Terry
Ionic Villa
Regent's Park
London, United Kingdom

27

ARCHITECTS

ROBERT ADAM

UNITED KINGDOM

"The creation of traditions, by deliberately preserving customs, by elaborating existing traditions or by inventing new traditions, is a direct product of change in society. This is done in order to preserve whatever is considered distinctive in a cultural group. It is the means by which society maintains its identity in the face of change. The creation of traditions is most noticeable in times of greatest change. Tradition, then, is not only a product of change, it can sit comfortably alongside the need to change. Modern life does not preclude tradition; the great changes we are experiencing seem rather to demand it."

RA

Robert Adam is a practising classicist with offices in the south of England. His designs have received awards in Britain and the United States and have appeared in major national and international exhibitions. His furniture and drawings feature in public collections. He has written two books – *Classical Architecture: a Complete Handbook* and *Buildings by Design* – and several papers on architecture and urban design.

Trained in London in the orthodox Modernism of the period, he discovered classical architecture through his reaction to the lack of historical context and the public rejection of the architecture of the period. He then won a scholarship to the British School at Rome.

His current commissions include the large development to the rear of the Ashmolean Museum for Oxford University presented here, the extension to Rhodes House in Oxford, village and urban design projects for the Duchy of Cornwall, restoration work and new buildings at Heveningham Hall, Suffolk, restoration work at other country houses and several new private houses.

In his advocacy of tradition, Robert Adam maintains that any claim to authen-

Extension to an old Manor House

Hampshire, United Kingdom

The design of this new classical extension to a medieval manor house contradicts the established rule that extensions to listed buildings should be more of the same. Behind an old farm house, where five centuries of history have created a mellow mixture of brickwork, timber and tile, is a dramatic new building in the classical style.

The effect is to preserve the identity of the old building while creating a striking feature in the landscape.

Opposite

Top: *The extension to the Manor House*

Bottom: *Overview of the Manor House*

Ashmolean Humanities Centre

Oxford, United Kingdom

The new large-scale buildings to be integrated into the Ashmolean Museum site comprise the Ashmolean Library, an imposing rotunda; a two-storey Cast Gallery focusing on a half-pantheon with an iron and glass dome; the Oxford Classics centre; the Griffith Institute of Egyptology with a new Gallery of 20th-century British Art on its top floor; various other centres; and a new central lecture theatre.

Above: *View with detailed section*
Opposite: *Interior view*

ticity is bound to fail, that the search for, historical accuracy is a chimera. He believes that it is possible to restore the cultural identity of the modern city "without seeking in vain to make people more like ancient Athenians or Renaissance Florentines." It is then possible to represent history rather than copy it, to recreate traditions. His approach is thus selective rather than comprehensive. He seeks ceremonial and symbolic elements that he can use to reconcile the past with the present, rather than attempting an integral representation of the past. He sees tradition as a bridge "between our ideals of the past and present reality".

JOHN BLATTEAU

USA

"Early Modern architecture came out of a craft tradition and its practitioners, such as Mies van der Rohe or Otto Wagner, were not afraid to use gold leaf or mosaic. The second generation of Modernists, however, in throwing out the Beaux-Arts system also threw out its resources. Consequently, there is very little understanding in the schools today about crafts; and students often don't realize how much they don't know. Architects now trust the head over the eye, losing sight of what architects are supposed to do, which is to make beautiful buildings."

J. B.

John Blatteau teaches at the University of Pennsylvania in Philadelphia, where he researches the nature of classical form and design. He is President of the Philadelphia Chapter of the Society of Architectural Historians and a member of the National Trust for Historic Preservation. An expert in the study of the repair, restoration and renovation of historic structures, he has a thorough understanding of building materials and how they behave through the life cycle of the building. His knowledge of traditional building techniques is outstanding. He lectures widely on the subject of classical architecture and his work has been exhibited in the United States and Europe.

John Blatteau also has a busy practice, focused essentially on institutional commissions. These include projects for the United States Government, the Brooklyn Botanic Gardens Master Planning and Administration Building, several buildings for Riggs Bank in and near Washington D.C., colleges, preparatory schools, churches, and hospitals. He won a limited competition to design the Benjamin Franklin State Dining Room at the Department of State. This room is the culmination of the suite of Classical American rooms that make

Riggs Bank, Northwest Office
Washington, DC, USA
The Riggs Bank Northwest Office is located in the historic Adams Morgans district. In line with the desire of the Bank to maintain a traditional image for all new buildings, this banking office blends with the classical fabric of the street. The simple, temple-like facade is a clear and recognizable symbol of stability and permanence. The pedimented entrance, supported by paired pilasters, has precedents in the temples of Delos. Elegant materials, such as granite bases, limestone walls and cornices and bronze doors enhance the sense of permanence.
Opposite
Top: *Detail of exterior*
Bottom: *Front elevation*

Riggs Bank, 808 17th Street
Washington DC, USA

This modern 12-storey office structure is next to the historic White House Precinct. The new interior architecture and space planning programme provide an interior in keeping with the surrounding historic district while integrating the demands of modern bank technology. The walls of the new lobby are of French limestone. The columns are of richly-coloured Italian marble with white Carrara bases.

Above
View of lobby
Opposite
Detail of lobby

up the State Department's official reception chambers. This opportunity allowed him to refine his ideas of what an ideal "Classical American style" might be, given the early history of the nation.

The Blatteau firm has established a long-standing relationship with Riggs National Bank, which has resulted in the restoration of the Bank's public offices and corporate headquarters as well as new construction. In all cases, the guiding principle for the architect has been to create functional working environments and memorable public spaces based on classical design principles.

John Blatteau believes deeply in "the enduring and timeless quality of classical architecture and its suitability in today's world," and continues to transmit that belief in buildings that are timeless and elegant.

Riggs Bank, Bethesda Office

Maryland, USA

A new English Georgian facade of limestone columns and entablature anchors this flagship branch of a rapidly-expanding Bank in the visual context of the community. Traditional elements express the continuity of an established, service-oriented bank. The volume of the banking hall is clearly marked on the exterior by large engaged columns, which flank two-storey windows. The main facade is clad with limestone, while a combination of brick and limestone makes up the side elevation.

The entrance and canopy are accented with ornamental bronze work. The banking hall establishes a strong visual image of stability through the accurate use of traditional classical elements. Plaster ornament and finely-detailed woodwork give character to the monumental interior. Varied ceiling heights, the teller screen and partitions combine to express the two different spheres of public and private interaction required in contemporary banking.

Opposite
View of facade
Above
View of interior

ALBERTO CASTRO NUNES
ANTONIO MARIA BRAGA

PORTUGAL

"Classicism relates to universal principles evolving out of vernacular expression and national experience. It imbues straightforward construction methods with the inspiration of experience, elevating them into an idealized realm in which symbolism and typology play a significant part. Classicism also has a rational authority verified over time, which translates the pragmatics of building into a timeless art. It involves a continuous historical dialogue between reason and tradition."

A. C. N. and A. M. B.

As natives of Lisbon and graduates of the Escola Superior de Belas Artes, both Alberto Castro Nunes and Antonio Maria Braga have had extensive exposure to the life of a dynamic city with many layers of history. They started their own firm in 1990, and have primarily been involved in the design of small-scale housing projects and public buildings. In both public and private realms, they have developed a coherent approach to the revival of vernacular and classical architecture in Portugal, looking to their own cultural background for models.

The Archaeological Museum in Odrinhas, designed in consultation with Leon Krier, clearly demonstrates their sensitivity to the complexity of those models, and the influence of each successive historical period. The ensemble – which is on the site of the oldest museum in Portugal that consists of a group of buildings which establish a pattern continuous with that of the village of Odrinhas.

Located not far from the town of Sintra, the museum took its inspiration from the well-preserved ruins of a Roman villa on the site. Nunes and Braga

National Film and Video Archive (ANIM)
Freixial, Portugal

This building for the storage and preservation of Portuguese and international film and video collections consists of several typologically independent units that are connected internally. The volumes articulate around several inner courtyards and both the architectural language and the resulting ensemble echo Portuguese rural manor houses and turn-of-the-century industrial buildings. The building technique is a compromise between traditional crafts and materials and construction in reinforced concrete to meet anti-earthquake regulations.

Opposite: *Views of the façade*

41

**National Film and Video
Archive (ANIM)**
Freixial, Portugal

Above
Aerial view
Right
View from portico

Opposite
Top: *View from balcony*
Bottom: *Interior*

have replicated the formal geometries, scale and materials of the villa to provide an evocative – but not literal – recreation of the past. Aware of the debate between those who advocate a more rigorously imitative approach, such as that of the J. Paul Getty Museum in Malibu, which reproduces Roman Villa form, and others such as Rafael Moneo, who simplified Roman construction techniques in his Mérida Museum, Castro Nunes and Braga have chosen the middle ground. They emphasize the virtuosity and exuberance of Roman planning, and the increasing confidence in creating space through engineering excellence that characterizes the best architecture of the Roman Empire.

JEREMY DIXON
AND EDWARD JONES
UNITED KINGDOM

"The architectural treatment of a building such as the Royal Opera House has to show an understanding of the difference between the square where it is located and the various surrounding streets. The project is too large to be treated as a single statement. The building is treated as a number of elements, each generating local elevations, which gives the appearance of a group of separate buildings. The classical style developed for the arcades that complete the square contrasts with the contemporary street elevations proposed for surrounding streets. Both internally and externally the challenge is to balance history and conservation against the need to recognize the new."

E. J.

Jeremy Dixon and Edward Jones, both graduates of the Architectural Association in London, first collaborated in 1972 when they won an international competition for Northamptonshire County Offices.

Jeremy Dixon went on to build a number of housing projects in London on sensitive infill sites, and won the competition for the Tate Gallery coffee shop; where he subsequently designed the restaurant too. In 1983, in association with Building Design Partnership, he was successful in an international selection process for the Royal Opera House, Covent Garden, and was one of six architects invited to submit schemes for the Sainsbury Wing of London's National Gallery.

Edward Jones won first prize in an international competition for Mississauga City Hall, Canada. His design won the Governor-General's Award.

They are again in partnership and currently working on a large number of commissions in the United Kingdom including the Royal Opera House, Covent Garden; student housing for Darwin College, Cambridge; a new science building for the University of Portsmouth; a master plan for Sainsbury PLC in

Royal Opera House
London, United Kingdom
This exciting scheme is a new chapter in the history of theatre design. It is also an important venture in coherent urban planning with the completion of the piazza – originally designed by Inigo Jones in the seventeenth century – as a complete and formal arcaded square. The challenge was to find an architectural approach that responded to the diverse contexts of the site bounded by the implied formality of the Market Square and by a series of typical Covent Garden streets with their ad hoc accumulation of architectural styles.
Opposite
Top: *A night view from the Square*
Bottom: *The Floral Hall foyer (Paintings by Carl Laubin.)*

Royal Opera House
London, United Kingdom

Above
The view from the Square
Opposite
A view from the portico
(Paintings by Carl Laubin.)

Bath; a shopping centre in St. Albans, and the regeneration of Bradford city centre. This gives an indication of the scope of their interests and concerns.

Despite the demands of such a busy practice, both partners remain committed to teaching and to the enhancement of their profession. Jeremy Dixon teaches at the Architectural Association and at the Royal College of Art, and lectures widely. Edward Jones was a senior tutor at the Royal College of Art for ten years, and has been a visiting professor at several colleges in North America including Harvard, Yale, Princeton and Rice, as well as in Italy. He is currently on the Architectural Association Council.

They bring deep insight and a unique a reading of historical continuity to their work, which exhibits an admirable balance between the demands of interpreting and restituting the architecture of the past.

RICHARD ECONOMAKIS
USA AND GREECE

"YES to the extension of towns and villages and cities on the basis of traditional criteria:
Unaltered urban fabric; correctly sized and scaled urban blocks; creation of neighbourhoods centring on squares and public spaces; integration of public, commercial and private functions; prevalence of pedestrian as opposed to vehicular streets and thoroughfares; healthy relationships of town and natural environment with maximum returns from preserved productive agricultural areas."

R. E.

Richard Economakis, now Assistant Professor of Architecture at the University of Notre Dame in the United States and previously Assistant Tutor at the Prince of Wales's Institute of Architecture in London, is one of the younger generation of classical architects. His experience includes five years as project architect and design associate with Demetri Porphyrios, and spells in the offices of John Simpson in London – where he was involved in the new designs for Paternoster Square – and of Allan Greenberg and Robert A.M. Stern in the United States.

He is a member of the Board of Directors of the Classical Architecture League, and has edited books - including *Acropolis Restoration*. He is currently Editor-in-Chief of *Civitas*, the newsletter of the Classical Architecture League.

His work was exhibited at the *Vision of Europe* Triennale in Bologna, Italy; the *Emerging Classical Architects* exhibition in Virginia; *The Art of Building Cities* in Chicago and *Urban Renaissance* in Bologna.

Economakis also co-authored the script for the documentary film *Nauplion: A City Besieged* (logos films) and has organized various conferences.

Centre for Classical Studies
Nisyros, Greece
This small museum and research centre is situated at the eastern end of Mandraki, opposite the ancient acropolis with its medieval monastery. It is conceived as an integral part of a future urban extension that will develop along existing roads and footpaths. Like the other large civic buildings, its forms are accretive rather than domineering, ensuring that the local urban scale is respected. Subtle formal inflections set up a dialogue with the public realm and are articulated by means of monumental features and architectural set-pieces.

Opposite
Top: *Perspective with diagrams*
Bottom: *Front and rear elevations*

ALLAN GREENBERG

USA

"Classical architecture provides us with a time-tested method of building beautiful cities; of creating noble civic, religious, and educational buildings that communicate humanitarian, ethical, and political ideals. The classical language of architecture is always modern because it is rooted in the physiology and psychology of the individual human... Classical architecture is both timeless and tied to a particular time and place. It is these qualities, together with those of democracy, urbanity, and continuity with the past, that continue to identify classical architecture as the appropriate language of architecture for the twentieth as well as the twenty-first centuries."

A. G.

Allan Greenberg was born in South Africa, and began his architectural studies in Johannesburg. After practical office experience in Europe in the early 1960s, he received his Master's Degree at Yale University, remaining in America to establish a private practice in Washington D.C. In parallel with his architectural career he has developed distinguished academic credentials, holding appointments at Yale, the University of Pennsylvania and Columbia University. He is considered to be one of the foremost experts on the work of Sir Edwin Lutyens, writing and lecturing about him extensively.

With his innate ability to adapt the canons of the past to modern times, Allan Greenberg has emerged as one of America's most respected classical architects. He is also one of the most meticulous architects working today and has succeeded in finding the craftsmen necessary to achieve the high level of finish he requires. He is perhaps best known for a succession of elegant country houses, mostly on large rural estates where the house is an integral part of a carefully-designed landscape setting. His scope ranges far wider than

Treaty Room Suite
Washington, DC, USA
The Treaty Room Suite of the White House consists of the elliptically-shaped Treaty Room and its two antechambers, two elevator halls and adjacent security lobbies, and two reception rooms for the Suites of the Secretary of State and the Deputy Secretary. Its curved walls are articulated by engaged columns with the Great Seal Order which was designed specifically for the State Department. It is a corinthian order with a capital incorporating the Great Seal of the United States; this is appropriate because the Secretary of State is the custodian of the seal.
Opposite
View of the Treaty Room

Deputy Secretary's Office
Washington, DC, USA

The suites of the Secretary and Deputy Secretary of State each consist of a formal office, private study, conference room, and large and small waiting rooms.

Their design was inspired by colonial and federal houses in Virginia and Maryland. These new rooms in the State Department's modern office building embody the ideals of American life and culture and reflect the continuity of American diplomacy.
Above: *View of the conference room*
Opposite: *View towards the Offices of the Secretary of State*

private houses, however, including such public commissions as the Treaty Room Suite and the offices of the Secretary and Deputy Secretary of State at the United States Department of State in Washington D.C.; the News Building in Athens, Georgia; several publishing offices, courthouses, churches, banks and a memorial, as well as furniture and interiors.

All are based on his belief that "classical architecture provides an organized system by which to enhance the life of the individual in society and to integrate buildings into cities and nature. Classical architecture's noblest achievements reinforce the best side of our natures as well as the ideals that help us to order our inner lives and our identities as members of a political community." In the words of Carroll William Westfall, Allan Greenberg's works "embody joyous, sensuous form, an underlying coherence of formal organization, and a wide range of references made fresh with intelligible and intelligent departures from expectations."

J. Wilson Newman Pavilion
Charlottesville, Virginia, USA

This classically-designed addition to Faulkner House, a mid-nineteenth-century listed building at the University of Virginia, acknowledges the restrained classicism of both Faulkner House and the architectural heritage of the region. It is a three-bay pavilion with a Tuscan portico, linked to the existing building by a new, two-storey hyphen, the upper storey of which is a three-bay glazed colonnade resting on a brick base.

Above: *View of facade*

Huckleberry House
Connecticut, USA

Huckleberry House was created for a couple who loved dancing and wished to have a two-storey domed ballroom as the central element of the plan. The plan is cross-axial, with the sun room and porch at opposite ends. They are identical except that one is glazed and the other open. The exterior is faced with yellow stucco with window units set within recessed arches.

Opposite
Top: *View of front facade*
Bottom: *View of rear facade*

Tercentenary Hall,
College of William and Mary

Williamsburg, Virginia, USA

The three-storey mass of Tercentenary Hall relates to neighbouring older buildings of the 1920-1950 period, but its architecture looks further back, to the nearby Wren Building and to the late seventeenth and early eighteenth century English architecture that is the source of much of the best American colonial design.

Above: *Lobby of the auditorium*

Right: *Auditorium*

Opposite

Elevations

Residence in Greenwich

Connecticut, USA

The plan is based on an "X" or chiastic form which architects in the late nineteenth century called a "sun trap" plan. Most of the principal rooms occupy ends of the "X", allowing each room to have windows on three sides and providing natural light and views of the marshlands.

Above: *Front facade*

Right: *Entry court*

Opposite

Stairhall

Overleaf

View of garden elevation from across swimming pool

Beechwoods

New England, USA

The five-part plan of Beechwoods is based on Palladio's Villa Badoer, and on American houses of the eighteenth to early nineteenth century, like Tryon Place and Monticello. The porticos at the entrance and garden sides of the house have a doric order and the dormer windows are incorporated into the regular rhythm of the metopes of the entablature.

Above: *View from the garden*

Right: *Front door*

Opposite

Stair hall

Overleaf

Overall view

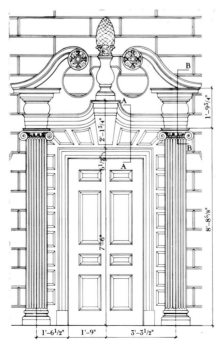

The Art of
PAUL GAUGUIN

HAMMOND BEEBY
AND BABKA

USA

"The Greek city grew around its raised holy place where the gods of the natural world had been gathered from the sacred groves and mountains. The goddesses and warrior gods rested in temples where the beauty of nature was idealized and transformed into an ornamental language of evocative beauty. Myth and life were one in these cities constructed in a spiritually charged landscape, but as humans became more confident in their power, the gods retreated further into the landscape, and the city emerged."

T. B.

As the lead design partner of the firm, Thomas H. Beeby oversees the progress of each project in the office through the design development phase and continues to monitor original creative intent through frequent review with the project team, material selection and detailing. His personal stamp is unmistakable: a balance of strength and original flair, combined with a liberal reading of classical conventions which enhances their spirit. This may be seen in a wide variety of projects produced by the firm, including museums and libraries, university building projects, theatres, urban and campus master plans, suburban office buildings, religious buildings, private residences and the restoration of historic structures.

This has been achieved in spite of Tom Beeby's extensive commitment to architectural education. He was Dean of the Yale University School of Architecture from 1985 to 1991 and continues his involvement there as a professor. Prior to that, he was Director of the School of Architecture at the University of Illinois in Chicago. He lectures frequently at universities throughout the United States and internationally.

Art Institute of Chicago, Daniel F. and Ada L. Rice Building
Illinois, USA

This three-storey addition to the Art Institute provides exhibition and storage facilities for four curatorial departments and houses the largest special exhibition space of any art museum in America. The two-storey skylit sculpture court surrounded by galleries orients the visitor. Walls are plaster with plaster mouldings. The wood trim and door frames are painted. The fluted columns in the sculpture court are in scagliola plaster; the flooring is Dolomite limestone and terrazzo.

Opposite
The sculpture court

**Art Institute of Chicago,
Daniel F. and Ada L. Rice
Building**

Illinois, USA

*The detailing in the new wing, such
as the scale and position of the
mouldings, reflects the sensibility of
the 1893 Shepley Rutan & Coolidge-
designed building.*

Above: *View of the galleries*

Opposite

Top: *View of the limestone entrance
facade*

Bottom: *Architectural details*

He is a Fellow of the American Institute of Architects, has served on the National Steering Committee on Design and has received the profession's highest design award for six projects, most recently for his participation in the Paternoster Square Redevelopment, in 1994. This was part of a master plan for the redevelopment of a seven-acre site near St. Paul's Cathedral in the City of London, restoring a traditional street plan to this district. His contribution was the design of two buildings, comprising office and retail space. The entire Paternoster plan is notable for its seamless combination of individual design efforts, and Beeby's addition to the project is exemplary in this regard.

The work of this firm manages to balance singularity of vision with the canons of classicism in a way that compromises neither.

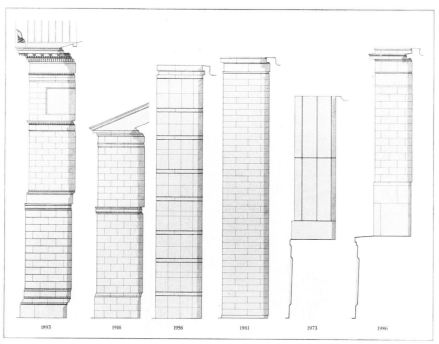

1893   1916   1956   1961   1973   1986

MANUEL IÑIGUEZ AND ALBERTO USTARROZ

SPAIN

"The ideal city, contained in the archetype of the polis of Plato, as described in his Republic, and put into practice by Hippodamus of Miletus, constitutes a clear example of the creative potential of the human spirit. Critical thought on temporal experience is certainly both necessary and useful in times such as our own. This is a task that requires both a democratic spirit and a profound philosophical study of urban planning ."

M. I. et A. U.

Alberto Ustarroz and Manuel Iñiguez are both from Pamplona and were instrumental in founding the San Sebastian School of Architecture. Following a series of early, private houses their work has expanded into the urban realm, focusing on the nature of the city and its institutions, particularly as related to the classical *polis*. Their plan for a new town near the monastery of Iratxe marked the beginning of the process, followed by their involvement in the restoration of the Baroque village of Lesaka, including the main square and a medical centre. This led to their participation in the restoration of the Royal Palace in Pamplona, and the reconstruction of its ramparts, and to an extensive new Sporting Complex beside the Arga River.

International commissions have allowed them to test their principles. These include a project to expand the facilities of the Château Pichon-Longueville and the planning of an "educational village" on the island of Kea in Greece.

More recently, they have returned to their origins in restoring the Plaza de la Compañia in Pamplona.

Château Pichon-Longueville
Pauillac, France
This project is conceived on a civic scale as befits its institutional status. The basic concept was to preserve the emblematic presence of the neo-renaissance château, the symbol of one of the greatest vineyards in the Médoc, and to establish a new visual and organizational axis.
The eighteenth-century walls, including the facades of a cuverie, an orangerie and a tower have been incorporated into a new order.
The entrance arc is designed as a belvedere for viewing the spectacular facade, mirrored in a large pool.
Opposite
Top: *Aerial view*
Bottom: *View of the courtyard*

ROB KRIER

AUSTRIA AND GERMANY

"My conviction is that in our modern cities we have lost sight of the traditional understanding of urban space. The cause of this loss is familiar to all city dwellers who are aware of their environment, sensitive enough to compare the town planning achievements of the present and the past, and have the strength of character to pronounce sentence on the way things have gone..."

R.K.

Rob Krier has exhaustively examined the components that made the traditional city memorable and convivial before the damage inflicted by the twin juggernauts of war and the modernist aesthetic. He concludes that "every period in history forms a unit with its own internal logic, which cannot be fragmented and interchanged with elements of other periods at will."

In America, architects such as Andres Duany and Elizabeth Plater-Zyberk revert to ordinances to restore a humane dimension to towns and cities. The same goal has led Rob Krier to seek typological elements that consistently recur in the history of the city. Emphasizing the connection between Classicism and Rationalism, he has been searching for a system that will allow him to understand and reconstruct the most compelling aspects of the traditional city. To do this, he has divided the urban area into public and private spheres; to these there correspond formal and informal behaviour patterns which show an underlying similarity.

His detailed historical study shows that the organization of public space

Breitenfurterstrasse
Vienna, Austria

This residential complex by Krier, Wachberger and Gebhart is based on classical concepts. It forms part of a general renewal of housing in Vienna which dates back to the beginning of the eighties. The arrangement of the various units is defined by the terrain and the need to create a physical and aesthetic inter-relationship. The volumes are organized in classical manner and given an up-to-date treatment.

Opposite
Front facade

Schinkelplatz
Berlin, Germany
Above: *A square enclosed on all sides against the derelict surrounds.*

Rauchstrasse
Berlin, Germany
New housing in individual buildings completed by a crescent.
Opposite
Top: *The crescent*

Ritterstrasse
Berlin, Germany
Small groups of housing that allow people to get to know their neighbours.
Opposite
Bottom: *View from the garden*

has always exercised a powerful influence on private architecture, especially that of the house. This echoes Jaquelin Robertson's conclusion, reiterated by other architects with a historical perspective, such as Robert Venturi, that the house is a city in microcosm.

Rob Krier's urban typology has made a definitive contribution to the study of civic space, allowing the best elements of the traditional city to be reconstructed. His architectural realisations, particularly those in Berlin, show how effectively a clearly articulated theory can be embodied in buildings.

Kirchsteigfeld

Potsdam, Germany

The guiding principle of the design for this new town of seven to ten thousand inhabitants is the urban village. The design was planned around the preserved Hirtengraben in the centre of the site, the Preisterallee with its wonderful avenue of ancient oaks, and a clean industrial estate bordering the motorway to act as a noise barrier and to provide jobs for the inhabitants. Another main concern was to achieve the best possible connections with Drewitz to the west and an estate of detached houses to the north.

The project is divided into two clearly defined areas, to the north and south of the Hirtengraben; a main square opens up right in the middle of each, and this is where the main cultural and commercial facilities are located. Each building will be designed by a different architect. The plan is organized in such a way that Kirchsteigfeld can become an independent town at any time but has good transport links with Postdam.

Opposite
and pages 78 to 81
Overall views
Above: *Detail of a facade*
Right: *Facades*

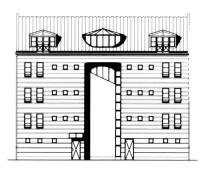

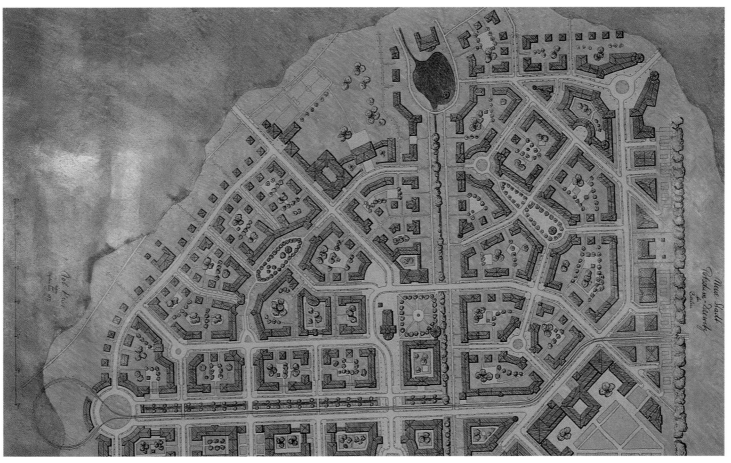

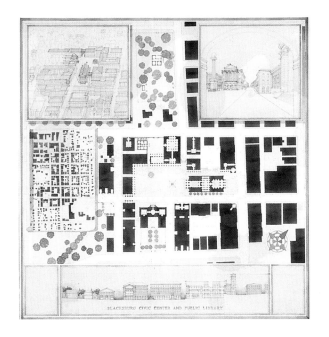

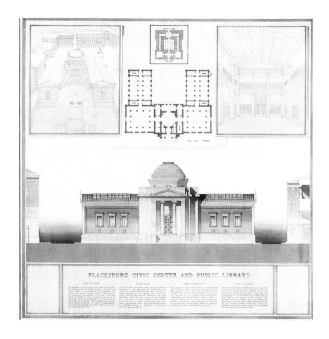

BLACKSBURG CIVIC CENTER AND PUBLIC LIBRARY

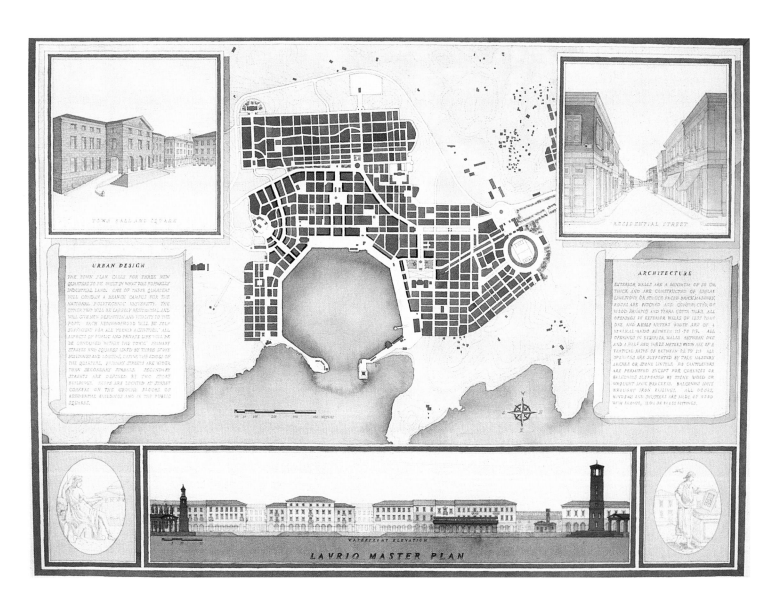

URBAN DESIGN

THE TOWN PLAN CALLS FOR THREE NEW
QUARTERS TO BE BUILT IN WHAT WAS FORMERLY
INDUSTRIAL LAND. ONE OF THESE QUARTERS
WILL CONTAIN A BRANCH CAMPUS FOR THE
NATIONAL POLYTECHNIC UNIVERSITY. THE
OTHER TWO WILL BE LARGELY RESIDENTIAL AND
WILL GIVE NEW DEFINITION AND VITALITY TO THE
PORT. EACH NEIGHBORHOOD WILL BE SELF
SUFFICIENT FOR ALL WEEKLY ACTIVITIES. ALL
ASPECTS OF PUBLIC AND PRIVATE LIFE WILL BE
CONTAINED WITHIN THE TOWN. PRIMARY
STREETS AND SQUARES LINED BY THREE STORY
BUILDINGS AND LOGGIAS, DEFINE THE EDGES OF
THE QUARTERS. PRIMARY STREETS ARE WIDER
THAN SECONDARY STREETS. SECONDARY
STREETS ARE DEFINED BY TWO STORY
BUILDINGS. SHOPS ARE LOCATED AT STREET
CORNERS ON THE GROUND FLOOR OF
RESIDENTIAL BUILDINGS AND IN THE PUBLIC
SQUARES.

ARCHITECTURE

EXTERIOR WALLS ARE A MINIMUM OF 50 CM.
THICK AND ARE CONSTRUCTED OF ASHLAR
LIMESTONE OR STUCCO FACED BRICK MASONRY.
ROOFS ARE PITCHED AND CONSTRUCTED OF
WOOD FRAMING AND TERRA COTTA TILES. ALL
OPENINGS IN EXTERIOR WALLS OF LESS THAN
ONE AND A HALF METERS WIDTH ARE OF A
VERTICAL RATIO BETWEEN 1:1 TO 1:3. ALL
OPENINGS IN EXTERIOR WALLS BETWEEN ONE
AND A HALF AND THREE METERS WIDTH ARE OF A
VERTICAL RATIO OF BETWEEN 1:2 TO 1:3. ALL
OPENINGS ARE SUPPORTED BY TRUE MASONRY
ARCHES OR STONE LINTELS. NO CANTILEVERS
ARE PERMITTED EXCEPT FOR CORNICES OR
BALCONIES SUPPORTED BY STONE WOOD OR
WROUGHT IRON BRACKETS. BALCONIES HAVE
WROUGHT IRON RAILINGS. ALL DOORS,
WINDOWS AND SHUTTERS ARE MADE OF WOOD
WITH BRONZE, IRON OR BRASS FITTINGS.

WATERFRONT ELEVATION

LAVRIO MASTER PLAN

MICHAEL LYKOUDIS
USA

"We feel that today architecture is at a crossroads. It is time for architects to contribute again towards a genuinely civic social structure; a meaningful built environment in which to conduct our lives. The surviving traditional city and its architecture present an alternative model that is rooted in and embodies civic and democratic life. Its language is legible to all. Traditional buildings and towns remain useful long after their original function has disappeared. We can see this in cities around the world where the urban fabric is hundreds of years old yet has adapted well to new uses and has accommodated new technologies ."

M. L.

Michael Lykoudis is an academic and practising architect in both the United States and Greece. He is co-founder and President of the Classical Architecture League, which has its headquarters in Washington, D.C. He has organised various conferences and exhibitions – including "The Art of Building Cities" in Chicago – lectures extensively and writes on architecture, exhibitions and books for the specialised and general press.

After studying at Cornell University and the University of Illinois, he practised first in Florida, then with Allan Greenberg in Washington, before founding his own practice. He has taught at the University of Notre Dame since 1991 as Associate Professor and Assistant Chair of the School of Architecture.

The two projects presented here – the Blacksburg Civic Centre and Public Library, on which he collaborated with Jason Montgomery, and the Lavrio Masterplan – manifest a preoccupation with the relationship between form, function and ornament exemplified in the studied applications of the classical language found throughout his work.

Civic Centre and Public Library
Blacksburg, Indiana, USA
A project based on the principles of the traditional city and its architecture.
Opposite
Top left: *Aerial view, view from the street, site plan and site elevation of the Civic Centre*
Top right: *Aerial view, ground floor plan, interior view and front elevation of the Library*

Lavrio Masterplan
Greece
A project to give new architectural definition to a decaying port city.
Opposite
Bottom: *The square and the street, site plan and site elevation.*

BRUNO MINARDI
ITALY

"The urban villa, understood as a one-family house with independent garden, has contributed to the definition of the residential areas of the modern city. In the past, entire parts of the city were progressively built up of urban villas: Victorian London serves as an example. However, in recent times the lack of norms and rational points of reference for projects has inevitably led to a loss of identity and to confusion on the outskirts of our cities. I am convinced that repetition must be the point of reference for any correct approach to the construction of a city."

B. M.

With offices in both Ravenna and Milan, and a post as professor of architectural design in Venice, Bruno Minardi is at the centre of a strong didactic axis, but he has avoided direct alignment with it. His earlier work, particularly in the 1980s, displayed some affinities with didactic architecture, and his evocative drawings of a utopian "Città Europea" (1984) reflect his concern with the present urban condition and with ways of improving it. Minardi specialises in large-scale planning, and these individual projects are somewhat exceptional.

Both the Casa Morigi and the Villa Trombini indicate a slight shift in his concerns. Located in the centre of old Ravenna, the Casa Morigi is a small building which replaced an existing house of little historical value. In its place Minardi has built "an ensemble of quotations": Verona marble window frames, metal grilles and an old doorway in stone taken from the ruins of a demolished house. He has also used traditional materials and colours. The decision to replace rather than restore is frequently controversial and Minardi has created a replacement that will serve as documentation of the past.

Casa Morigi
Ravenna, Italy
The unifying thread in this house (designed by Bruno Minardi with Lorenzo Zaganelli) is the use of simple forms, precisely-crafted details and materials traditional to Ravenna. Inside, four columns of red Verona marble define the rhythm of the internal spaces. The new house is fully integrated into the old centre by skilful use of the local tradition.
Opposite
Facade
Overleaf
The courtyard
Page 89
Interior views of hallway, stairwell, living room and bathroom

Villa Trombini

Marina di Ravenna, Italy

In the design of this villa, Bruno Minardi and Lorenzo Zaganelli have paid special attention to elements of the urban villa and, more specifically, villas in seaside resorts: garden, porticos, terraces, towers, layout, materials, decor, finishing and colours. Within this well-established formal repertory, it has been possible to make choices and propose new solutions and variations. The result is a building in harmony with its urban context.

The Villa Trombini, in contrast, stands in a large garden by the sea. The tower typical of seaside houses in the region is replicated in the crenellated core of the house. A deep arcade has been used for similar reasons. The otherwise shallow relief is slightly accentuated by restricting the exterior palette to pale green and white. This villa is an effective study on how to evoke history without transcribing it literally.

Villa Trombini

Opposite

The balcony

Overleaf

Main facade

LIAM O'CONNOR
UNITED KINGDOM

"Very little has changed since Roman times concerning the building of a house. The use of local materials, necessitated by the inconvenience of moving heavy materials over long distances, makes as much sense today as it always has done. Ideas about the vernacular tradition in building are therefore not solely the province of historians but belong in architectural practice... They are the concern of those who still believe that the Vitruvian triad of firmness, commodity and delight are as appropriate today as they have ever been."

L. O'C.

Liam O'Connor was Leon Krier's assistant before setting up his own architectural practice in 1989. Since then he has co-edited the *Vision of Europe* catalogue and exhibition in Italy and won two international competitions: an urban design competition for the centre of Warsaw, Poland; and one for three buildings in the rue de Laeken in the centre of Brussels, Belgium, winning an honorary prize in the European Award for the Reconstruction of the City.

Formely adjunct professor at the University of Notre Dame in Indiana, USA, and in Rome, he now teaches at the Prince of Wales's Institute for Architecture. He has published and exhibited projects at numerous galleries, including several Royal Academy Summer Exhibitions. He edited the book "Viterbo – Santa Maria in gradi" for the Prince of Wales's Institute.

Since 1994, he has been Special Adviser to the Secretary of State for the Environment on Architecture and Urban Design. He has designed and built projects ranging from single family houses to apartment buildings, offices and buildings for educational use.

House in Belgravia
London, United Kingdom
This new house in Belgravia, in the centre of London, successfully blends into the existing architecture of the street; it does not disturb the pattern of the street but retains its own individual character. The traditional materials used throughout contribute to this harmonious appearance. It is built in solid loadbearing brickwork and faced in stucco. The portico is in stone and based on the order used for the Tower of the Winds in Athens.

Opposite
Top: *Perspective of street facade*
Bottom: *Street elevation*

Sundridge Park

Kent, United Kingdom

As part of a masterplan drawn up for the whole estate, several projects have been completed, including this new wing built onto the mansion originally designed by John Nash and set in landscape gardens designed by Humphrey Repton.

The two-storey stuccoed building is divided into two parts connected by a tower in which the staircase is housed.

Opposite

Top: *Exterior view of the extension*
Bottom: *Sundridge Park*
(Painting by James Hart Dyke.)

Above
Details showing the relationship between the extension and the main building

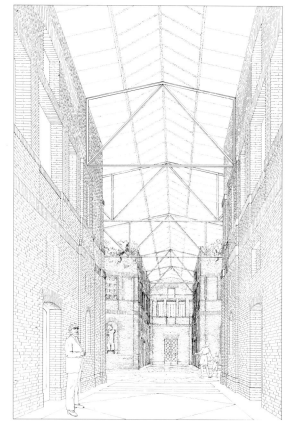

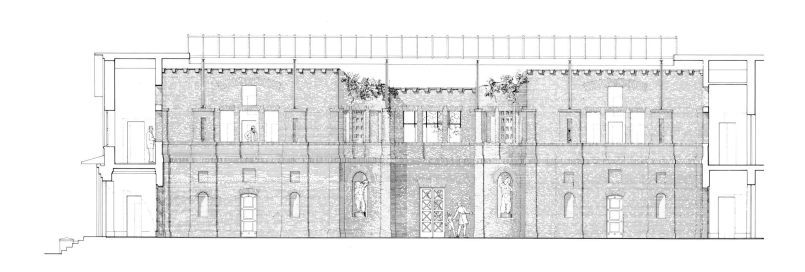

HELMUT RUDOLF PEUKER

GERMANY

"The rules of architecture have changed very little over the past 5000 years. The materials used for constructing houses can be counted on the fingers of two hands and yet they open up a unique richness of form, colour, surface and smell. Traditional architecture is based on the perception that a house is a house and not the object of any new invention or the result of a designer's originality. Unfortunately, the results of many designers' experiments are there to insult our eyes for many decades to come."

H. P.

After studying architecture at the technical universities of Braunschweig and Aachen, Helmut Peuker spent a year in Rome and a further two years doing research on Renaissance architecture at the Max-Planck-Institute for the History of Art there before opening his own architecture studio in Munich in 1988. One of his first buildings, which won an open competition and which we show here, was for the Livos company.

For this building he made full use of his research. Measurements and reconstructions of antique and Renaissance buildings always emphasize the importance of anthropomorphic measures such as the Roman palmo (1 palmo romano = 0.2234 m). Almost all the measurements in the Livos Hall derive from the palmo and its multiples. The width and height of the gallery floor are 20 and 40 palmi respectively, and form a ratio of 1:2. The diameter of the rotunda is 50 palmi and its four niches are large enough to surround a human being of normal height (4.5 palmi wide by 10 palmi high).

Other projects include apartment houses in Berlin-Köpenick, the rebuilding of a classical house and the reconstruction of a neo-renaissance building.

Building Livos

Emern, Germany

The Livos hall is a former furniture factory transformed into a new administration building. To allow light from the existing skylight into the building, the ceiling between the ground and first floor was removed. A rotunda was combined with a gallery space on a roman cross to create a round space for meetings, receptions, concerts and exhibitions. On the first floor a corridor leads around the hall, its upper windows opening onto the inner space.

The strong vertical character of the resulting space is tempered by deep horizontal joints between the bricks.

Opposite

Interior views and longitudinal section

DEMETRI PORPHYRIOS
UNITED KINGDOM

"Of the various architectures that have flourished over the ages, the architecture of Greek antiquity best exemplifies the idea of tectonic order."

"Architecture is neither the arbitrary adornment of building nor the inevitable causal outcome of building technique. Rather, it is the symbolic form that man gives to his building craft. Architecture makes us see the building craft from which it is born, from which it detaches itself as art, and to which it always alludes."

D. P.

Demetri Porphyrios has explored the connection between vernacular and classical architecture more thoroughly than most, in both theory and practice. He has consistently maintained that Classicism is not a style because it is neither arbitrary adornment nor mere fashion. "In those things we call classical we recognize a kind of timeless present that is contemporaneous and at ease with every historical period." For Porphyrios, the emphasis is on the origins of architecture as shelter and on the representational value of tectonics.

His projects span both architecture and urban design, from the early didactic pavilions at Highgate and the Belvedere Village near Ascot to the new quadrangle at Magdalen College, Oxford, the Brindleyplace office buildings in Birmingham or the village of Pitiousa on the island of Spetses in Greece. All his work is characterized by an unerring instinct for appropriate materials – generally indigenous and natural – harmonious proportions and contextual sensitivity.

Belvedere Village, near Ascot, for example, is a grouping of farm buildings, cottages and stables, built around three main spaces which provide continuity

New Longwall Quadrangle, Magdalen College
Oxford, United Kingdom
The new quadrangle re-affirms the urban quality of the adjacent quads while opening up towards the deer park. The residential units are broken down into small units with maximum views of the Great Tower. All residential accommodation is organized in the traditional Oxford stairs and sets with two or four rooms per landing.
The buildings have traditional masonry walls with ashlar Ketton stone externally and painted plaster inside. All exposed timber is oak. Roofs are in stone tiles except those of the arcade and tower, which are lead.
Opposite
Aerial view

New Longwall Quadrangle, Magdalen College

Oxford, United Kingdom

Buildings of different character and scale co-exist in harmony with the landscape.

Above, opposite and overleaf:
Views of the Quadrangle and entrance tower

and an urban structure. The village of Pitiousa is a sympathetic extension to the old town of Spetses; the new buildings draw knowingly on the vernacular and classical architecture of the island. Differences in colour, the treatment of certain profiles and the design of entrance gates introduce variety, while maintaining a pleasing overall urban cohesion.

For Porphyrios, Classicism is a living tradition, open to adaptation and interpretation, and responsive to region, climate and nature. It has evolved from

and coexisted with the vernacular. "The work of Porphyrios," writes Paolo Portoghesi, "has a quality of creativity which finds itself not in academic repetitions but in a classicism treated as a way of life."

Three Brindleyplace

Birmingham, United Kingdom

Around a central atrium rises a seven-storey building onto which three other volumes are articulated. To the south west, the arcaded fronton with loggia faces the Square. To the north east, the tower rises from the centre of the urban block and serves as a beacon for the whole Brindleyplace development as seen from the canal and along Sheepcote Street and beyond. To the north, a low U-shaped volume modulates the scale of the building as it unfolds towards the canal. The main entrance is off Brindley Square via a double height arcade leading into a lofty foyer, which in turn opens onto the central glazed atrium. This is the heart of the building, revealing at once its organization in plan and section.

The atrium includes a perimeter arcade at ground floor level.

At every office level, the lifts open onto generous balconies overlooking the atrium.

Above
View from the canal
Opposite
View from Brindley Square

JAQUELIN ROBERTSON
USA

"Somehow our culture – indeed all cultures exposed to the Western industrial commercial virus – has apparently lost not just a comprehensive language of city building, but any recognition of the necessity of such a language. Since architecture is made up of a number of long-established, if continually changing languages, each with its own rudimentary laws of form and structure, urban design, which is the aggregation of various specific architectures, is a kind of generalized, even crude, meta-language. That is, the city is a language of languages, also with its own rules."

J. R.

Jaquelin Robertson is an architect and urban planner who has written eloquently about the connections between these two disciplines. He was a founder of the New York Urban Design Group and has served as a New York City Planning Commissioner. He founded his architectural firm in 1978, forming a partnership with Peter Eisenman in 1980.

He has served as Dean of the School of Architecture and Commonwealth Professor at the University of Virginia and is a founding member of the Jeffersonian Restoration Board in Charlottesville, Virginia.

In his writings, Robertson frequently recars to Thomas Jefferson's University of Virginia. He analyzes what he calls the "exaggerated presence,": the overscaled classical language used by Jefferson, which, though refined, was responsive to the needs of a new country trying to make its mark in a vast continental landscape. He extends this idea to Latrobe's Capitol Building, which "stands out monumentally against the surrounding Arcadia, reaffirming the timeless authority of the Classical old world in the new."

New Albany Clubhouse
Columbus, Ohio, USA
The Clubhouse is conceived as a large country house in the manner of eighteenth-century Virginia. It acts as a social and recreational centre for a 27-hole golf course designed by Jack Nicklaus. Clad in hand-moulded red brick, the building is accented by limestone and capped by roofs of copper and slate. It commands sweeping views of the golf course.
Its one-storey sports club has broad porches, clapboard and board-and-batten siding, with overhanging roofs that evoke the rustic character typical of the outbuildings of many of America's great houses.
Opposite
Exterior views of the clubhouse

New Albany

Columbus, Ohio, USA

As well as designing the Clubhouse, Bath and Tennis Club, Cooper, Robertson & Partners were responsible for the master plan of this new 5,000 acre development. They also designed four signature residences to set the style for subsequent residential development. Taken together these illustrate various themes of Georgian three- and five-part organization, volumes and proportions. Finely articulated fences of wood and brick line the semi-private street.

Opposite

Signature residences

Ertegun Residence

Southampton, USA

This weekend country villa is timber framed, and sheathed in cedar siding painted a rich saffron colour with white trim; the roof is raised seam copper. It is both formal and cosy (for four or fifty guests), has a single-storey top-lit great room flanked by two-storey wings, and provides space for a collection of grand and vernacular paintings and furniture.

Above

View of the facade

Overleaf

Detail of facade, view from the rear garden and view of swimming pool

JOHN SIMPSON

UNITED KINGDOM

"If Classical Architecture is to become part of the mainstream once again, part of the Classical Architect's aim — duty even — must be to instigate and influence a process of change within the construction industry. A change which step-by-step, as more and more architects bring pressure to bear on the building industry through their designs, will bring mainstream construction into line with the requirements of Classical architecture. Unfortunately, thanks to the Modern Movement, we now have a largely unskilled workforce, and a legacy of industrialized construction with which to work, with all its inherent defects and shortcomings."

J. S.

Soon after graduating from the Bartlett School of Architecture of London University, John Simpson set up his practice in London specialising in urban design and classical and traditional architecture. He is involved in all levels of design from creating whole towns and villages to designing furniture and fittings. He has demonstrated that the Classical tradition can accommodate contemporary economic, technical and functional requirements, while creating architecture and spaces whose scale, organization and form are in tune with modern life.

As well as running his own practice, he teaches at the Prince of Wales's Institute of Architecture and was part of the team working on Paternoster Square in the City of London, as well as on the Poundbury development in Dorset where work is due to start shortly on his market building.

Simpson is concerned that his architecture be durable and functional. He believes that Classical ideals, which he calls "the Greater Principles of Architecture", provide the basis for timeless building, since "If the building is intended to be there for ever, the fact that it is built properly will be of very

Country house
Sussex, United Kingdom
A small country house, compact and practical for everyday use, but with the grace and proportions of an eighteenth-century residence. The building is square in plan with each facade responding to its orientation and internal layout. It has a Palladian symmetrical plan arranged round a two-storey roof-lit domed central hall with an octoganol library on the upper level. The design of the facade revealed by the approach from the north is a paraphrase of a triumphal arch. All the interior furnishings and some of the furniture were designed by the architect.
Opposite
View of the front facade

Country house
Sussex, United Kingdom
Opposite
View of staircase
Above
View of lightwell

high importance." He is not averse to technology, believing that if used properly, it can be liberating, and serve the architecture it supports. But he is convinced that the link between traditional construction methods and the traditional city are much closer than people realize. " The growth of contextualism as an acceptable mainstream approach, particularly in the context of the European city with its tight medieval origins, has, hand in hand with the rise in conservation, provided an enormous boost to traditional construction." The rise of the green movement and the growing awareness of energy conservation have also played their part. The most encouraging development is that new towns in Britain, such as Poundbury, are being built with these traditional urban characteristics.

Country house

Sussex, United Kingdom

Above:

View of vestibule

Opposite

Top: *The drawing room*

Bottom: *The music room*

116

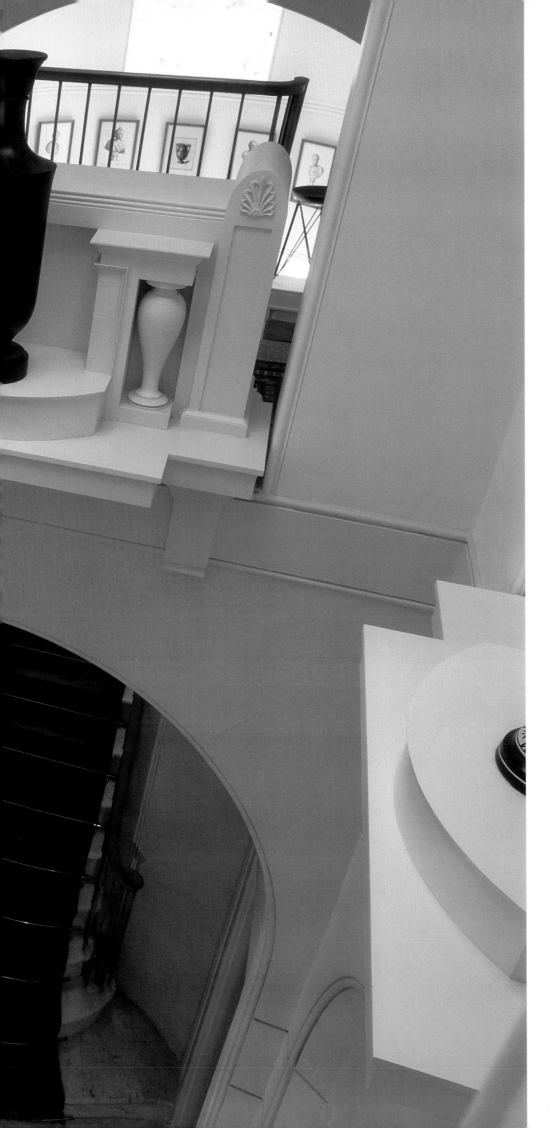

Country house
Sussex, United Kingdom

Left Stairwell:
Overleaf
Views of back room from the stair-case, and from the garden
Pages 122-123
View of the house from the rear garden

London Bridge City

London, United Kingdom

This design is for the second phase of a development covering an area of land opposite the Tower of London along the southern bank of the River Thames between London Bridge and Tower Bridge.

With the demise of the Pool of London, all commercial activity in this area disappeared. The new plan therefore tackles the changing nature of London's riverside and makes the riverbank a public amenity for Londoners to enjoy. It was therefore necessary to change the perception of the buildings. In general the streets and the scale of the proposed buildings are similar to the old warehouses, and the arrangement of the urban blocks recreates the grain of the area – but in a less utilitarian manner – by providing a series of new public places and squares.

The site provides office and retail space and restaurants.

Above

The view from the Tower of London (Painting by Carl Laubin.)

Opposite

Top: *Aerial view of the model*

Bottom: *Drawing of the view from London Bridge*

Country house

United Kingdom

The design of this house for the King and Queen of Jordan creates an asymmetrical composition with colonnades, two new wings and a tower.

It contains a large hall with trussed timber roof, state reception rooms and living quarters.

The construction is traditional, using load-bearing brick and Portland stone. The brick is stuccoed and painted. The roof is in green Westmorland slate.

Above

Views of front and rear of the house

Lime Street

London, United Kingdom

The new building of this commercial and retail development adjacent to the historic Leadenhall Market in the City of London forms the southern boundary of the Leadenhall Market Conservation area adjacent to the Victorian extensions to the market. The site is also part of the Roman basilica forum that once formed the heart of Londinium. The new building forms the centrepiece of the view through the main arched entrance of Leadenhall Market and has been designed to respond to its location. The tail of the building pulls away from the market creating a square around the market. An arcade is incorporated within this facade to complement the market buildings. Shops and cafés along the arcade entice pedestrians to the market beyond.

The building is brick with stone dressing. It has a copper roof with bronze embellishment. The urn at the apex of the roof is a chimney. The masonry is self supporting.

Opposite

The view from inside the galleria (Painting by Carl Laubin.)

THOMAS GORDON SMITH
USA

"When I began to incorporate elements of classical architecture in my designs, I used them for formal and cultural reasons...I have now gained a deeper understanding of how the elements can be articulated to express concepts as well as to achieve a formal synthesis. I have begun to grasp a paradox inherent in the tradition of the elements of classical architecture which has confirmed my conviction that they are appropriate to use today. In terms of form and meaning the elements of classical architecture are extremely flexible. Even when they are contradicted, they remain comprehensible in relation to the tradition.."

T. G. S.

Thomas Gordon Smith practises and teaches in Indiana, where he is chair of the School of Architecture at the University of Notre Dame. He is a former winner of the Rome Prize, an exhibitor at the highly significant Presence of the Past exhibition at the Venice Biennale at the recent exhibitions in Chicago and Bologna, and the author of *Classical Architecture, Rule and Invention* (a standard work on the subject), and of studies of Greek architecture and nineteenth-century furniture. Recently he coordinated an architectural programme in St. Petersburg renforcing cooperation between the St. Petersburg Academy and the Prince of Wales's Institute of Architecture.

Smith's buildings include the Kulb House in Illinois, renovations and additions to the School of Architecture at the University of Notre Dame and a Civic Centre for Cathedral City in California.

Thomas Gordon Smith is best known for his emphasis on the duality present in our classical heritage. Very few ruins of ancient Greek architecture have retained their original polychrome decoration. Indeed, until the early nineteenth century, it was assumed that they were designed in white marble.

Vitruvian House
South Bend, Indiana, USA
This house was designed for the architect and his family. The exterior form is indebted to a type of European and American house of the early nineteenth century with a prominent temple flanked by lower wings. It was often used in the American north-east and mid-west in the thirties and forties. Here, this regional influence is merged with Palladian and Vitruvian overtones to develop a new Grecian typology. The Ionic central block contains the entrance hall and oecus with a twenty-two foot groin-vaulted ceiling.
Opposite
View of front facade; detail of portico

As travel became easier and the number of site surveys increased, it became clear that they were in vivid, primary colours that were even more pronounced in the clear light of Greece. Smith addresses this issue head on.

He also considers that controversial issue of historical accuracy. Purists contend that the state of modern research permits the detailed reproduction of the classical canon. Others argue that this view does not respect the spirit of the language. Time has passed, conditions have changed, and detailed imitation is no longer appropriate. The clarity of Thomas Gordon Smith's vision makes his contribution to this debate essential.

Vitruvian House

South Bend, Indiana, USA

*The volumes are divided between a
central temple front and the one-
storey wings. The Ionic central block
is built in brick and limestone. The
exterior articulation of the wings is
Doric with terracotta metopes,
representing the labours of Heracles
and reliefs of each of the animals he
encountered.*

Opposite
View of front facade
Above
View of dining room
Overleaf
View of drawing room

FRANÇOIS SPOERRY
FRANCE

"What I have tried to do is to find a clear connection between popular architecture which varies so very much across the world, and modern architectural technique; to discover common traits, familiar points of reference, and the underlying structural characteristics of cities and villages – these points of reference are neither modern nor ancient, they are timeless. Modern techniques have replaced traditional architectural styles and can be held responsible for spoiling the beauty of both town and countryside."

F. S.

As a result of the devastation of urban areas and the resulting critical shortage of housing stock after the Second World War, many architects found work in reconstruction projects as well as the more publicized new building initiatives. François Spoerry set up a practice in Mulhouse and, as a town planner, concentrated on the city centre there. In the early 50s, he designed several new residential complexes and one of the highest buildings in France, a tower in Nancy.

By 1960, the replacement of tho pre-war urban fabric by large, open plazas and anonymous tower blocks – endemic throughout Europe – had convinced him of the sterility of modernism. He became what he describes as "a keen supporter of a more human concept of architecture." His love of coastal villages and the sea led him to study the vernacular traditions of these areas, generally spared by wartime bombing. This led to his design for the "lagoon city" of Port Grimaud, intended as both an alternative model of community planning and a commercial development. It was inspired by his love of the Greek islands.

Port-Grimaud
France
Port Grimaud was born out of a passion for sailing ships and a love of the sea. In this aerial view, the church, the town-hall and Market Square can be seen at the centre with the many peninsulas radiating from them. Each is bordered by houses with "their feet in the water" and their boats moored in front of them. Seven kilometres of canals wind through the town. They are designed so that yachts can be moored astern to their own jetties and the four-metre foundations on which the houses are built were specially designed to match the jetties. Only large yachts moor at the public quay.
Opposite
Aerial view

Port-Grimaud

France

From the outset it was decided that each house would have a view over the water, that cars would be banished, and underground galleries would house all technical services, thus avoiding such adjuncts as telegraph poles and television aerials. Volumes, colours, and gently sloping roofs all add to the harmony.

Opposite

The roofs of Port-Grimaud

Above

Aerial view

Pages 138 to 141

Houses and details

His skill at making a completely new town look as if it had, like other coastal villages, slowly evolved over hundreds of years, brought him world-wide acclaim. Port Grimaud became the standard for other architects wishing to replicate historical precedents. Spoerry's passion for the integration of architecture with the environment is evident, as is the harmony between buildings and water. The commercial success of Port Grimaud allowed Spoerry to expand his ideas; proposals for Hainan Island, China and Miyakohima Island, Japan, came soon afterwards.

One of his most exciting projects is what he calls his "Great American Project", Port Liberté, a lagoon-city just a stone's throw from Manhattan.

At offices in Mulhouse and Port Grimaud, Spoerry and his team of architects and planners continue to pursue his vision of a humane marriage between architecture and nature in all aspects of urban life.

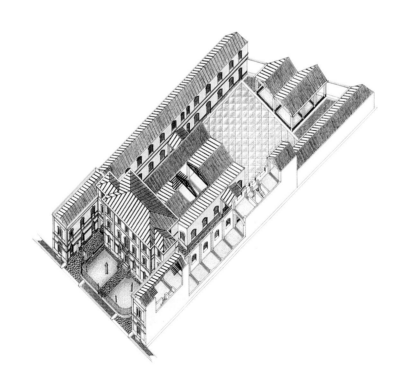

TAGLIAVENTI
AND ASSOCIATES
ITALY

"History advanced from ruins and from people anxiously searching for cultural continuity rather than a definitive breakdown with a Past that they felt extremely close and present despite its temporal distance. From that rather uncertain framework, the Classical age we now call the Renaissance was born. Now, on the eve of the third millennium, a new group of architects, historians and philosophers is again beginning to reflect on the ideas of continuity and the relevance of tradition."

G. T.

Ivo Tagliaventi, the paternal half of this father and son team, graduated from the Institute of Architecture and Urbanism in Bologna and was strongly influenced by the organic approach to architecture. He collaborated with James Stirling on the new urban centre of Bologna and was involved in the planning of Zola Predosa, a suburb of Bologna, and the design and construction of its new Town Hall. He is a member of the Town Planning Committee of Florence, and has served as President of the "Vision of Europe" Committee.

Gabriele Tagliaventi also graduated from Bologna and is now a professor at the University of Parma. He has organized seminars on traditional town planning and classical architecture with Leon Krier and Maurice Culot. He won first prizes in the competitions for the Rue de Laeken and the Reconstruction of the Warsaw City Core. He has also published several books on traditional town planning including *A Vision of Europe* (1992), and *Urban Renaissance* (1996).

The work presented here reveals the dedication of this partnership to the re-creation of the best of the past, and their continuing ability to convert their extensive joint knowledge of the history of the city into reality.

Mixed urban complex
Bologna, Italy
This reconstruction and extension project accommodates some 3000 sq.m. of residential, commercial and office space in a traditional lot on the boulevards that surround the historic centre of Bologna.
The design of the new buildings adopts the architectural features of Bologna's commercial and industrial buildings of the early twentieth century, ensuring that this urban block, which was destroyed during World War II and suffered from later modernist interventions, once again forms part of the coherent urban streetscape of the centre of Bologna.
Opposite
Top: *View from the courtyard*
Bottom: *Axonometric*

QUINLAN TERRY

UNITED KINGDOM

"The great thing about traditional building is that it leads inevitably to architecture. If you allow yourself to design within the constraints imposed by traditional materials and construction ... you will very soon discover the wisdom of the historic styles. For Classicism is a search for a universally valid form of architecture and, of course, if something is universally valid, it is valid at all times. In this sense you are always doing something that has been done before.... If we want a future for our grandchildren, I propose that we build traditional buildings."

Q. T.

Quinlan Terry in both his buildings and his writing has done much to dispel public misunderstanding about Classical architecture. His Richmond Riverside complex, perhaps his best known project in Britain, has proved that Classicism is not only commercially viable but popular too. He has been able to achieve such an effective synthesis because of his realistic assessment of the strengths of the approach he is using. His "Seven Misunderstandings about Classical Architecture" refutes the critics of classical style.

The first misunderstanding is that Classical architecture is pastiche. But in the *Quattro Libri* of Palladio, no guidance is given as to size, scale, materials and construction. The architect cannot simply construct according to a formula; creativity and resourcefulness are indispensable.

Modernists claim that function implies form, but Terry argues that classical language is symbolic; where form also implies function, both design and interpretation are facilitated. Another criticism relates to the new uses to which the traditional language is put; Terry points to the versatility of Classical architecture.

St Helen's Bishopsgate
London, United Kingdom
This very popular church in the city of London was twice bombed by the IRA. The building was damaged but remained standing.
This restoration returns the church to a simpler pre-Victorian form and lay-out with medieval and Georgian details and proportions.
The additions include a new West gallery (inspired by an early engraving) and staircase, a new East window with remnants of the stained glass shattered by the bomb worked into the tracery, and a new door made in Portland stone on which all the mouldings are hand carved.
Opposite
Interior view

Howard Court, Downing College

Cambridge, United Kingdom

This student residence is the completion of a design conceived some time ago. As planned, it continues the Doric order of the Lecture Building with a fluted Palladian Doric colonnade supporting the rooms above with a very large Tuscan overhanging cornice. The window is Venetian.

Above:
Drawing of overall view
Opposite
View from portico
Overleaf
Overall view

Next, he stresses the durability and lower maintenance cost of natural materials in comparison with their industrial counterparts. The fact that "they give pleasure to the eye and make us feel a good, simple pleasure in natural things" is an added bonus.

Fifthly, on cost, he points to savings in energy costs: "In the past, resources were scarce, and buildings reflected moderation." There is also a misunderstanding about the availability and expense of crafts and trades today. But "the truth is that whenever there is good work to be done, there are people available to do it at competitive rates."

Lastly, regarding its political implications, he responds that Classicism has represented so many political and religious systems throughout history that all the "spiritual, political, material and temporal influences are crystallised in classical forms, rendering the grammar neutral.".

Maitland Robinson Library
Downing College

Cambridge, United Kingdom

The new library is built on the principle that the books are stacked in the centre of the plan. The resulting square building has an octagonal staircase that provides access between basement, ground and first floors. The entrance doorcase is a combination of Greek key pattern with splayed architraves.

Opposite
Interior of the dome showing the Downing Griffin

Above
Front facade

Right
Drawing of a facade

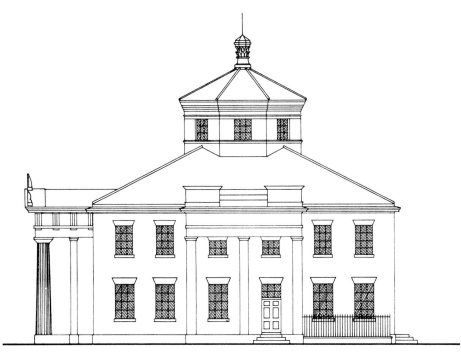

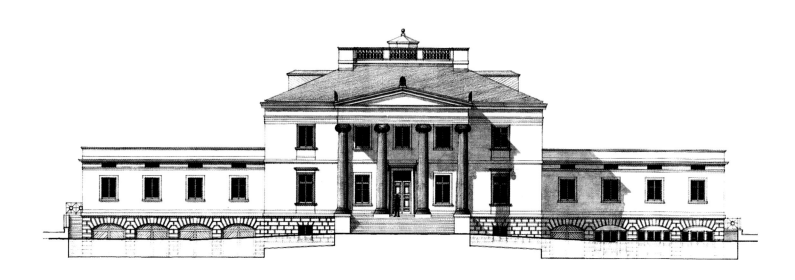

A New House

Frankfurt, Germany

The architecture here is modern classicism with no capitals, mouldings or orders. At the beginning of the design process, it was an English classical house but as it proceeded it gradually moved away from Palladio towards Schinkel. It has a central hall and porticoes and owes a stylistic debt to the Greek Ionic order preferred by Schinkel.

Above
Front elevation
Right
Rear elevation

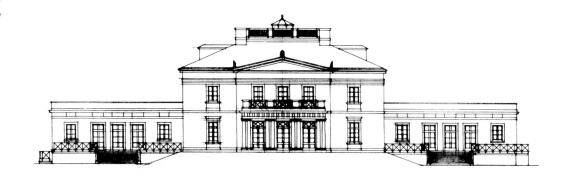

Ionic Villa, Regent's Park

London, United Kingdom

The Ionic Villa is one of six villas for the Crown Estate Commissioners in Regent's Park, London on a site sloping down to the Regent's canal. It is based on a design by Andrea Palladio for Girolamo Ragona at Le Ghissole, published in the Quattro Libri, *but the plan has an early Georgian treatment. The materials used are loadbearing brick with stone dressings, faced in stucco.*

Above
Front facade

Right
Front elevation

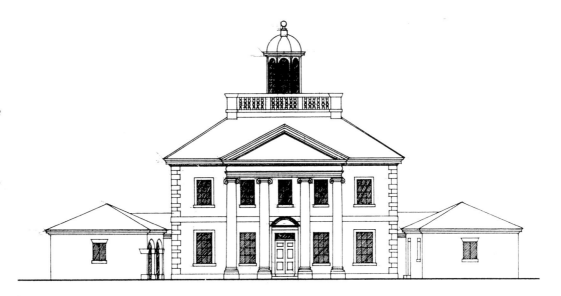

Ionic Villa, Regent's Park

London, United Kingdom

All the villas continue the picturesque tradition established by John Nash in the early part of the nineteenth century.

The Ionic Villa is at the broadest end of the site. The plan therefore has a narrow front with more depth than the other villas. It employs a giant order with four columns and is massive in scale.

Opposite

View of stairwell

Above: *Rear facade*

Right: *Rear elevation*

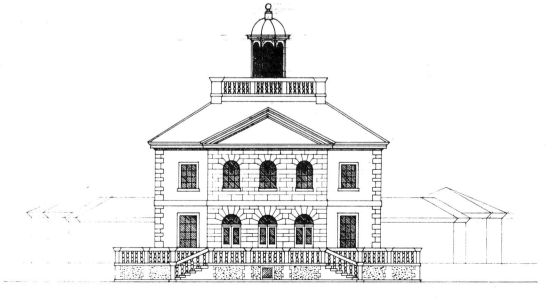

Veneto Villa, Regent's Park

London, United Kingdom

*The scale is smaller and more refined
than the Ionic Villa. It employs a
Doric order with a superimposed
Ionic order and parapet on eight
columns, inspired by the Cornaro
Loggia in Padua by Falconetto, and
other Palladian themes popular in
the Veneto. The plan is based on
Palladio's Villa Badoer. Internally,
the detail is English with a strong
Veneto influence.*

Opposite
View of staircase
Above: *Front facade*
Right: *Front elevation*

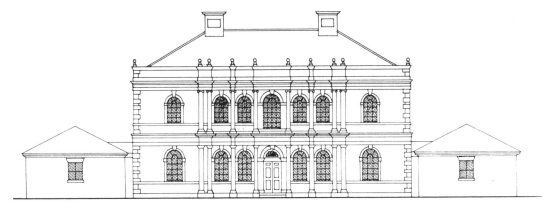

Gothick Villa, Regent's Park

London, United Kingdom

The plan is based on Palladio's Villa Saraceno but also reflects John Nash's preoccupation with Gothick style. The inspiration for much of the detailed work was Nash's Longner Hall and Combermere Abbey, Shropshire – which was one of the foremost Gothick buildings in the Strawberry Hill style – and a number of medieval East Anglian Churches.

Opposite

Front and rear facades

Above: *Views of the hall*

Right: *Front elevation*

URBANISM

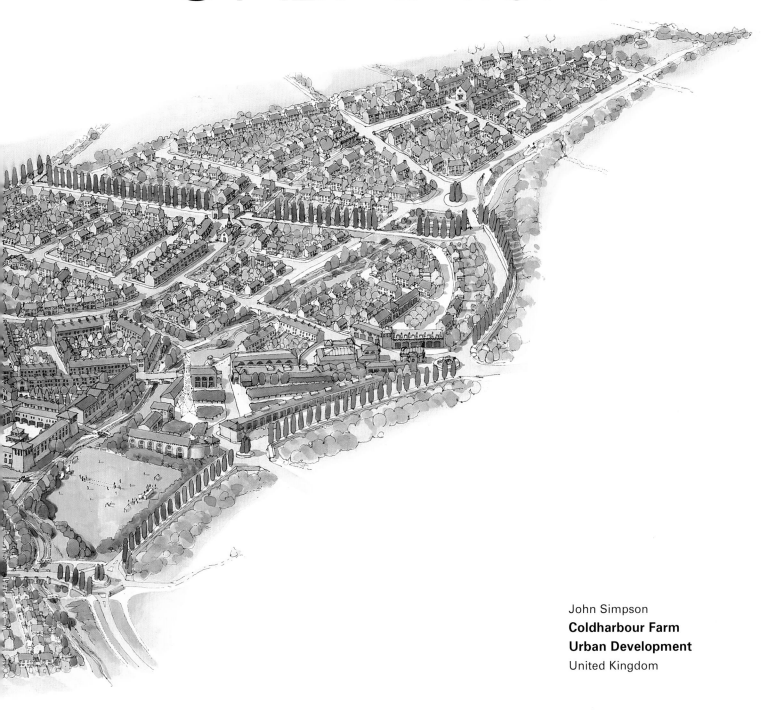

John Simpson
Coldharbour Farm
Urban Development
United Kingdom

LEON KRIER

ARCHITECTURE

CHOICE OR FATE*

If, suddenly, one day, by some inexplicable phenomenon, all the buildings, settlements, suburbs and structures created after 1945 – especially all those commonly called "modern" – suddenly disappeared, would we mourn their loss? Would the disappearance of prefabricated tower blocks, mass housing estates, commercial strips, business parks, motorway junctions, modular university campuses and schools, new towns, etc., destroy the identity of our favourite cities and landscapes?

If, on the other hand, some parallel phenomenon destroyed in one fell swoop the whole of our pre-World War II architectural heritage, especially all "historic" buildings, hamlets, villages, and cities, what impact would that have?

In terms of real estate volume, both heritages are approximately equal; comparing them, however, allows us to appreciate the fundamental differences in their nature: their specific symbolic, aesthetic, civilizing and emotional qualities, their power of attraction, identification and repulsion. Has so-called "modern" architecture, with its insatiable drive for autonomy, its cultivation of the *tabula rasa* approach and celebration of change and revolution, really liberated us from our "historic" past? Or has it made us more dependent?

Looking back over our experience of the past fifty years, can we honestly maintain that the architecture and urbanism of our time are in any way comparable in worth and achievement with those of other ages? It is true that a Baroque city needs no Gothic presence and that Renaissance towns can easily do without the vestiges of other eras. But is this true of recent settlements?

The Modern Movement may well claim to be the sole expression of its age; but has it lived up to its declared ambitions? Does the extraordinary technical and scientific creativity of the industrial age have a parallel in architecture and urbanism with respect to the aesthetic and symbolic expression of a practical, ecological intelligence?

Twentieth-century urbanism is just so many forms of "sub-urbanism" and the latter has become the symbol of the evils of society. But is there an art of building cities today? Are there towns that seduce and attract us, recently-built cities and villages where we would freely choose to live? Is there a true choice in architecture?

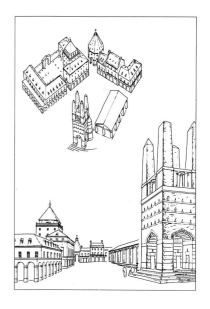

**Tower and market square,
Middle Farm quarter**
Poundbury, United Kingdom

Opposite
House at Seaside
Florida, USA

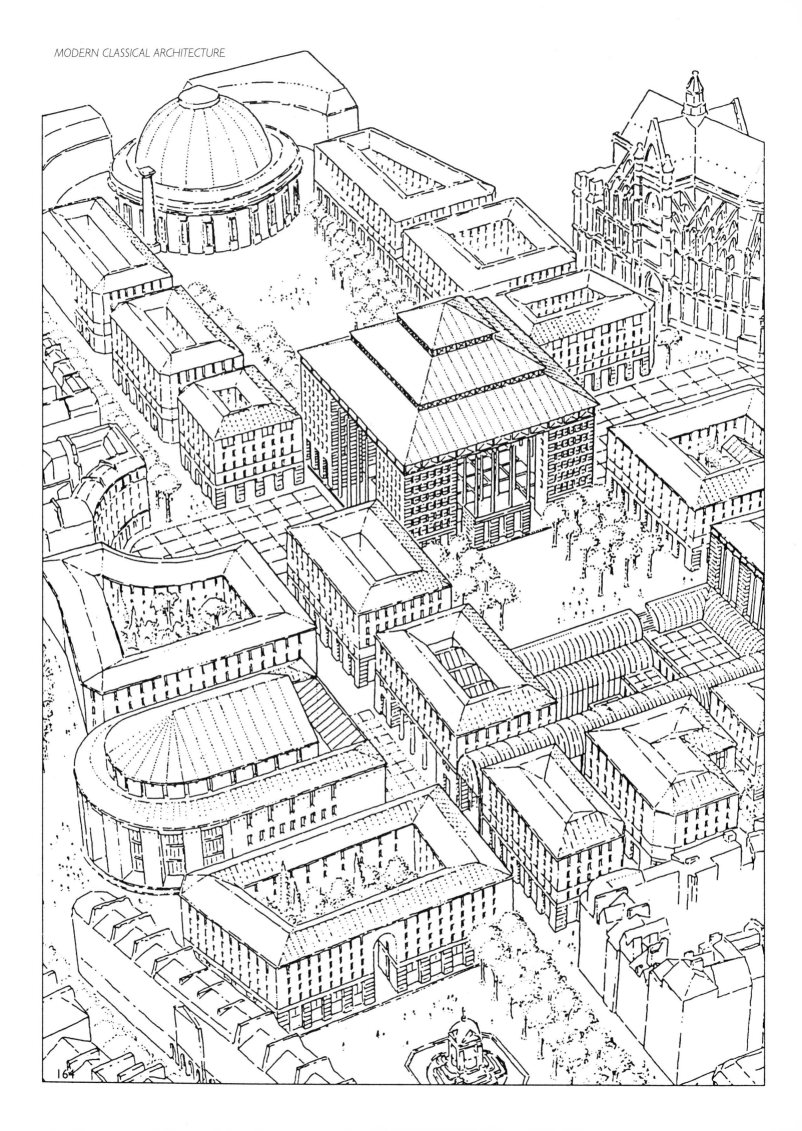

The Destiny of Traditional Architecture

Traditional architecture is not something that can be acquired once and for all. It is transmitted from individual to individual and varies greatly with each generation.

It can disintegrate suddenly after attaining great heights or it can flourish extraordinarily in a few short years, after a period of general decadence. Like all living organisms, it evolves.

Its present penury is not inevitable and does not justify its global rejection. Its very decadence creates the conditions necessary to clarify its causes and to prepare for a general improvement.

Architecture finds its highest expression in the classical orders. A legion of geniuses could not improve them, any more than they could improve the human body or its skeleton. Karl-Friedrich Schinkel drew the attention of his age to the fact that the progress in architecture had been so great in the past that only the most trained eye could detect any improvement in the classical orders.

This movement is evident at all cultural levels. A classical language is not abandoned because it is spoken badly; but, on the contrary, the instruments necessary to reestablish its classical form are recreated. The argument that the language of traditional architecture is spent and definitively obsolete was based not on any criticism of its internal structures, but on a rejection of its abuses and their political context. And yet, true traditional architecture still speaks to us. Far from being foreign to us, it serves us well. It conveys its essential messages to us, even if we are not capable of sending any.

It remains a living language, although many architects have lost the will to learn its grammar and to use its vocabulary. Past and present crises have neither eroded nor polluted the traditional language. Its rules, its meanings, its inventories and vocabularies are temporarily veiled in confusion. The transfer of its knowledge and its know-how has suffered a brutal interruption. A new apprenticeship and a reconstruction of its disciplines are possible. The transfer of values occurs neither mechanically nor involuntarily. It occurs through determination and reason: it is a cultural choice.

Arte Sacra Pavilion
Venice Biennale
(Painting by Rita Wolff.)

Preceding page
Les Halles
Paris, France

After modernism

A mere half century ago, the modernist movements claimed to have the definitive solutions to all the problems of the built environment. Today, one truth is evident: without traditional landscapes, cities and values, our environment would be a nightmare on a global scale. Modernism represents the negation of everything that makes architecture useful: no roof, no load-bearing walls, no columns, no arches, no vertical windows, no streets, no squares, no privacy, no grandeur, no decoration, no craftsmen, no history, no tradition.

Surely, the next step is to negate these negatives?

In fact, for several years now, the neo-modernists have had to admit that there is no true substitute for the traditional fabric of streets and squares, and yet they claim that urban planning must be based on modernist architecture.

Fifty years of modernism and thirty centuries of traditional architecture are today being compared and judged. But in fact, popular opinion will accept any city plan and skyline provided that its architecture is traditional. The eradication of the teaching of traditional architecture has not succeeded in eliminating either the need or desire for it or its use.

For three generations, modernist polemics have succeeded only in excluding traditional architecture from public commissions, and in reducing it to its lowest level in history.

In parallel, modernism produced its most horrific results when it was in complete control. It is not by chance that it produced its best results when it accounted for only a small part of architecture, as was the case in the twenties. This could also prove to be the case in the future.

False pluralism
No possibility of choice.

In the general barbarity of the machine that colonises cities and landscapes with mediocre dwellings and shelters, everyone is on the losing side. It is not a question of who will win the war, but of how to improve quality on all sides, by establishing intelligent, democratic competition, a pluralist education and non-partisan but effective criticism.

Present Prospects

After the violent criticisms and the almost total rejection of one type of modernism in architecture, a rejection culminating in the resounding speech of the Prince of Wales at Hampton Court in 1984, it appears that the establishment, in return for a few superficial adaptations of the product and its presentation, has taken complete control of public architecture. Today criticism and demonstrations rarely cause delays in major architectural and urban projects. There appears to be general resignation to a universally dominant architecture. But the absence of criticism does not necessarily indicate acceptance.

It is obvious that, apart from a few exceptions, modernist buildings are not in keeping with historic city centres: the Palais-Royal, the Maison carrée in Nîmes, the Louvre forecourt were not in need of their recent additions. We may well ask ourselves what improvement has been made... If these additions had been built in the suburbs, there would be scarcely a mention of them. However, millions of visitors are used as evidence of the exceptional popularity of ostentatious modernist projects, whereas the popularity of Port-Grimaud or Williamsburg is denounced as politically dangerous. It is perhaps absurd to force architects to design traditional facades in historic centres; but

True plurality
Freedom of choice.

Vraie PLURALITÉ
× LIBERTÉ DE CHOIX ×
LK 85

surely it is even more absurd to pretend that without world-shattering interventions historic centres lack vitality or dynamism?

In fact, there are two kinds of architecture. Public, standardised, international-style architecture that may be perceived as arrogant or even aggressive; and private architecture, often based on regional models, that blends naturally and harmoniously with the landscape.

The former is the product of public architecture, official commissions and competitions: generally symbolised by new towns, infrastructure and institutions (hospitals, schools, cultural and administrative centres).

The latter is always the result of private initiatives and includes individual houses and, more recently, leisure complexes in keeping with their region whether it be Virginia, Provence, New England, the Bahamas, Bavaria or Tuscany.

In the face of such an enormous democratic reality, the ideologists cannot ignore it but keep their distance by denouncing it. Instead of investing in this social phenomenon intelligently, instead of civilising it with criticism and education, they confine themselves to contempt. And yet in the advanced democratic countries, leisure architecture and the private residential sector are today dominated by traditional architecture.

The vast urban sites of Richmond Riverside and Poundbury in England, Port-Grimaud, Gassin and Plessis-Robinson in France, Seaside and Windsor in the United States, Florence-Novoli in Italy, Potsdam-Drewitz in Germany, Lomas de Marbella and la Heridia in Spain prove that large-scale modern infrastructure, even whole neighbourhoods, based on traditional architecture and urban planning that meet the needs of a developed industrial society can be built in very short periods. They may well be the first large examples of a serene and civic modernity that is not alienating, nor kitsch nor aggressive.

Opposite
Belvedere

The enduring principles of traditional architecture

The resurgence of traditional architecture only makes sense in the broad context of modern planning and infrastructure, cities, villages and countryside. And this is not contrary to the wishes of the majority of the democratic electorate. Traditional architecture has continued to serve in all ages and under many political regimes; there is no reason why this should not be the case in the future. Such towns and buildings can be adapted, with imagination and elegance, to the changing needs of an advanced industrial society. That was

the case with the railway stations built in the nineteenth century... Even the functions of an air terminal or an aeroplane hangar are not in contradiction with the typology and building techniques of traditional architecture. We are not asking the air terminal to fly, and a modern hangar can be seen as an enormous portico. The way a garage is built has nothing to do with the car inside!

And so there is no practical or philosophical reason for imposing modernist solutions when traditional methods have proved their superiority financially, technically, typologically and aesthetically.

The assertion that the principles of traditional architecture have been made obsolete by industrial technology is arbitrary.

In architecture – as in other ancient disciplines such as mathematics, gastronomy or philosophy – technical, formal and typological innovation cannot be a goal in itself. The reduction or extension of the typological or morphological inventory of architecture is not achieved by the work of a genius or by individuals, but by changes in use, customs, materials, and techniques.

The creativity, the individual quality, the originality of traditional sites and buildings lies in the adaptation of a panoply of forms and plans to very different local conditions.

Traditional architecture is a pure invention of the mind. It has greater universality than language, for its elements are comprehensible to people everywhere without any translation. Independently of country and age, it includes all buildings designed by artisanal and artistic cultures. Such cultures are all based on individual, autonomous trades, in contrast with industrial organization and production.

Traditional architecture produces objects with a very long life that are fundamentally different from the objects for immediate consumption of modernism. It is for this reason that its principles, its forms, its techniques resist fashion for, to paraphrase Hannah Arendt, no public space strictly speaking, no collective culture is possible without the potential immortality of our buildings and our cities. There is no short-term wisdom.

Without such material and moral immortality, architecture cannot aspire to be a civic art, or the most important tool of civilization.

Classical Lycée
Design for an extension
Echternach, Luxembourg

*Text and illustrations are from *Architecture, Choice or Fate* by Léon Krier, published by Andreas Papadakis Publisher, London 1997. (Pages 13, 14, 15, 16, 79, 181, 182, 183.)

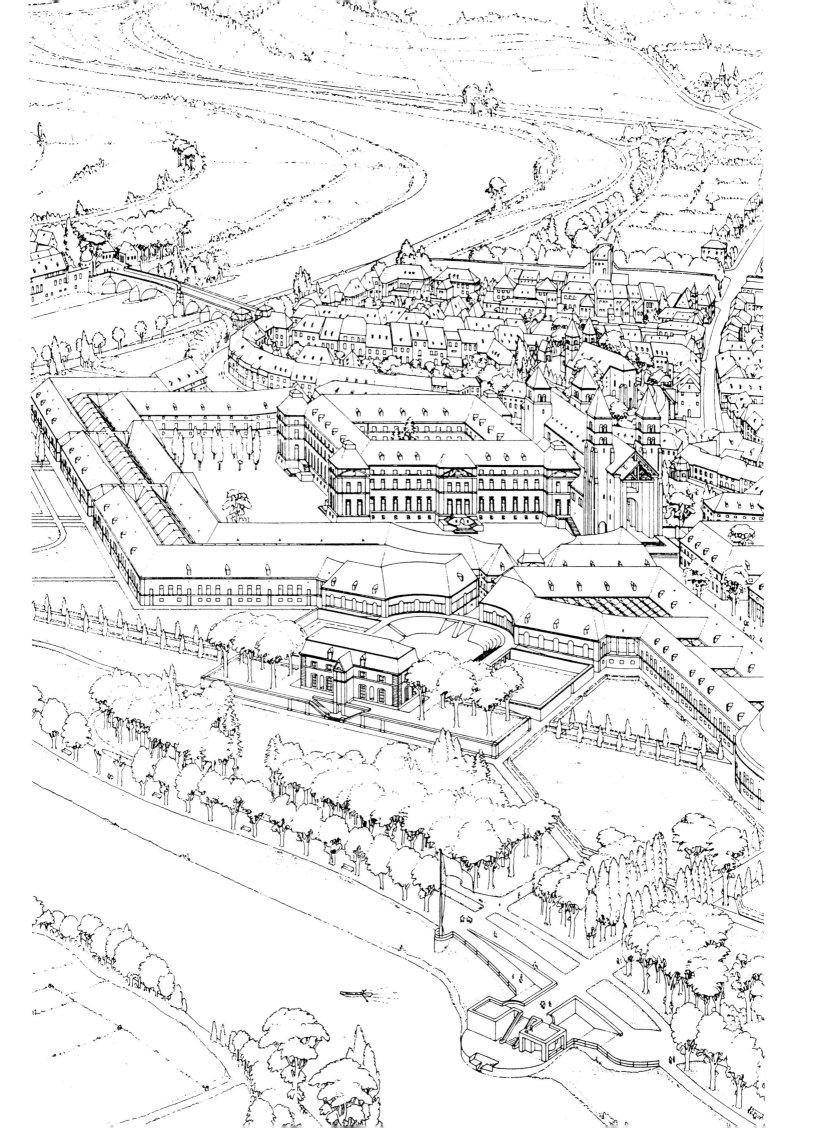

RUE DE LAEKEN

BRUSSELS, BELGIUM

"The completion of this project to reconstruct the Rue de Laeken is a sign of hope that we may at last be entering a new and more humane age of European urbanism." (His Royal Highness the Prince of Wales).

At the instigation of the *Fondation pour l'Architecture in Brussels,* a Europe-wide competition was organized in 1989 for the reconstruction of part of an historic Brussels street that had been destroyed in the 1960s. Over 200 entries were received. The critenon used by the international jury was that the projects should together create a street suitable for the heart of Brussels and for the people who would live there. The site is now under construction by architects from France, Spain, Belgium, Italy and the United Kingdom, all of whom are under forty years of age.

The real issue is one of architecture and urbanism: how to reconstruct a section of a street in a way that respects the scale and structure of the traditional city and the aesthetics of a historic street dominated by neo-classical language, while at the same time meeting the technical, functional and economic requirements of modern housing.

When the winners had been selected, the next task of the international jury, was to award each of the seven winning architects a lot or lots to rebuild, and to formulate recommendations for the further progress of the project. The

competition galvanized public attention. Its organizers firmly believed that this urban grouping would not only benefit the city of Brussels, but prove to other European cities that the variety of the past was not incompatible with contemporary requirements.

In response to widespread demolition in the urban core of Brussels after World War II, developers offered a site of this size would normally have designed a single multi-storey building. Given existing codes, this would have provided 12,000 square metres of residential space, or about one hundred apartments. By choosing instead to build a series of units, the potential size of the development was approximately halved. This did not make it financially unviable, however. The size of the buildings and the traditional building techniques made it much cheaper to construct, and since the apartments are of a higher standard than is usual in new buildings, they are in greater demand than other developments in the city, and can command higher rents.

Many difficulties had to be overcome by the architects in the design phase, including a city requirement for underground car parking - which made a load-bearing wall structure much more complicated - a request for lifts in the taller houses, and the need to adapt seventeenth-century details to meet twentieth century energy requirements. But the consistent high quality of the finished buildings is testimony to the architects' ingenuity.

In addition to houses, the development includes shops, offices, workshops and courtyards surrounding a large garden filled with trees and a fountain. In fact, it is this aspect of the complex that made the town houses viable, since all the pieces work together in a symbiotic way. The resulting street is an integral statement, despite the diverse personalities and nationalities of the architects involved.

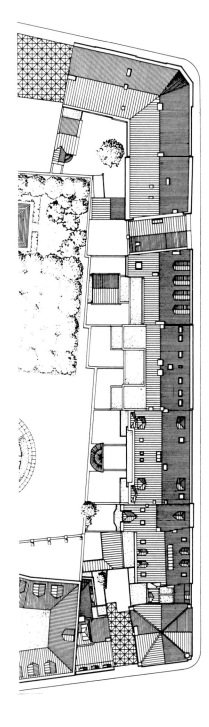

Rue de Laeken
Brussels, Belgium
Above
Roof plan of the street
Right
Street elevation

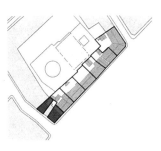

LOT 1
Gabriele Tagliaventi
and Associates
Italy

This five-storey tower at the corner of the rue de Laeken and the rue du Pont Neuf is a skilful conservation of a private house that sets the formal tone for the remainder of the units. "The design was inspired by a desire to announce the presence of a remarkable district dating from the early nineteenth century, a district that recounts the city's history, a tale of destruction and renewal."

Above and left
Tower house on the corner, and general perspective of the street
Opposite
View of the street

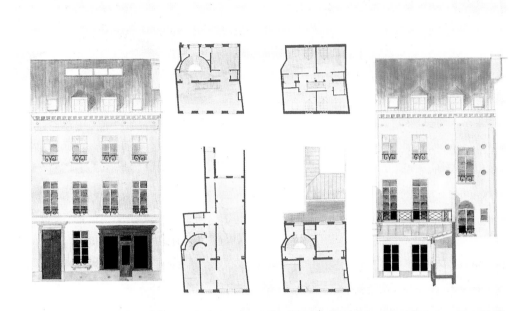

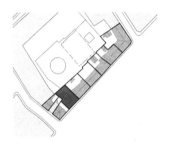

LOT 2
Atelier 55, Marc Heene and Michel Leloup
Belgium

This lot consisted of the identical reconstruction of an existing house which was too fragile to conserve (2a) and a tall, narrow house in the traditional Brussels style (2b). This, a one-family house, runs right through to the interior of the lot. It has two full floors and six half-floors arranged around a central wooden staircase - one of many devices that pay homage to Brussels architecture of the Art Nouveau period.

Above

Lot 2b: View of balcony on the main facade

Right

Facades and plans of Lot 2a; facades, plans and sections of Lot 2b

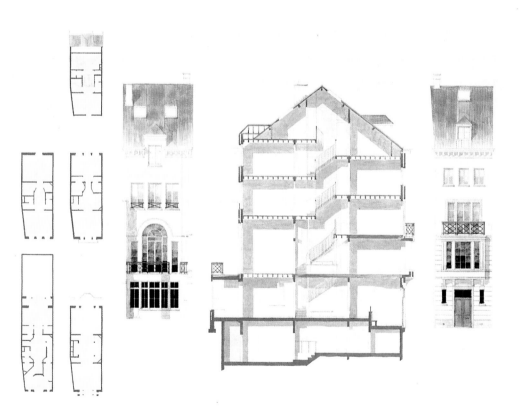

FAÇADE SUR LA RUE - ECHELLE OCₓₓₓₓ

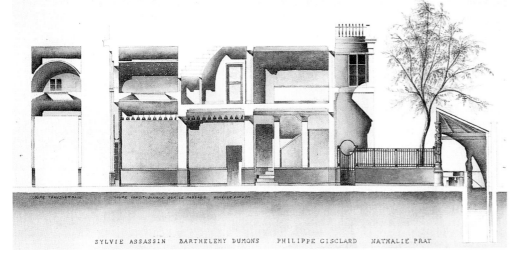

SYLVIE ASSASSIN   BARTHELEMY DUMONS   PHILIPPE GISCLARD   NATHALIE PRAT

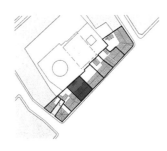

LOT 3
**Sylvie Assassin
and Barthélemy Dumons**
Spain
**Philippe Gisclard
and Nathalie Prat**
France

The elegance and originality of this project are evident on the ground floor in the arched passageway with its polychromatic decor and, in the background, the access pavilion to the underground parking area with its terracotta caryatid; on the second floor in the ambulatory on the garden side and the row of oculi looking across to the roofs of the old houses on the opposite side of the rue de Laeken.
Left
Top: *Facade and section through the passageway*
Bottom: *Detail of rear facade*

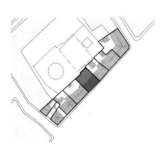

LOT 4
**Jean-Philippe Garric
and Valérie Nègre**
France

*Behind the thick walls of this
apparently massive facade is an
apartment building where the
rational plans and cross-sections, the
simplicity of
the volumes, and the architectural
vocabulary maximize potential rental
revenue without sacrificing the
variety of the individual apartments
or the originality of the whole.
Spaces are generous throughout,
especially the huge arched entrance
hall with its black and white decor.*

Right

Top: *Facade*

Bottom: *Axonometric of the ground
floor and mezzanine*

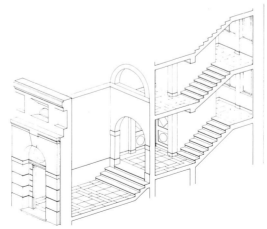

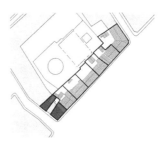

LOT 5
Javier Cenicacelaya
and Inigo Salona
Spain

A small adjacent house having been conserved, the lot is of irregular shape. To obtain right-angled rooms, the architects placed corridors along the separating wall, leaving the hall and stairwell intact. The size of the latter is emphasized by contrasting colours and the play of light.

Left
View of staircase from above

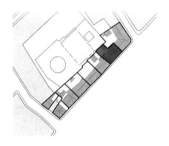

LOT 6
Liam O'Connor
and John Robins
United Kingdom

This lot is divided into two distinct projects that strictly respect the building line of two old houses. The gabled house has been rebuilt exactly as it was using elements from the original building. The other house has been given a public passageway through to the rear, highlighted with pilasters and finished in French stone. Inside, the plans are dominated by an impressive spiral staircase that runs between the three apartment floors.

Above
Rear facade
Right
Top: *Main facade*
Bottom: *Detail of the "identical" reconstruction*

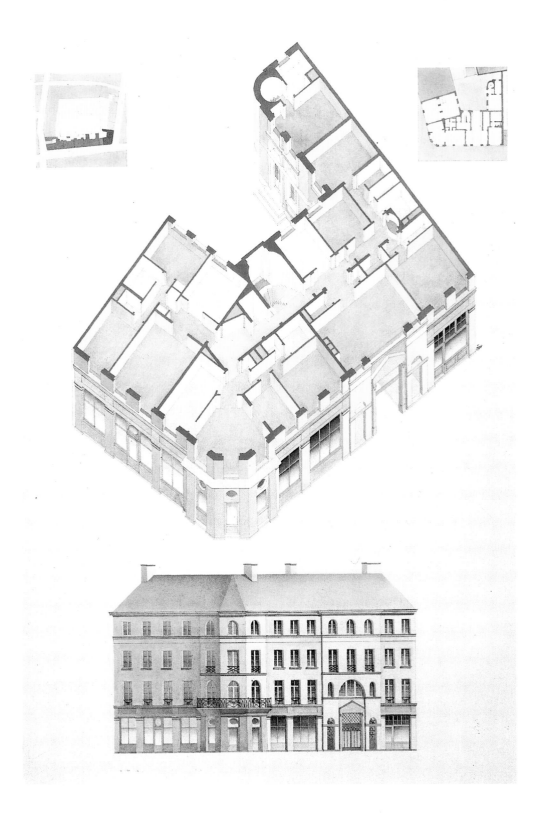

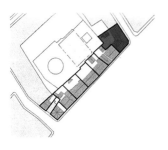

LOT 7
**Joseph Altuna
and Marie-Laure Petit**
France

This lot on the corner of the Rue de Laeken and Rue du Cirque was occupied by a house with various annexes and a narrow office building. The new apartment building continues the line of roofs and cornices, band mouldings and bay windows.

The layout of the large apartments is French in style, as is the U-shape of the central courtyard, which also provides access for pedestrians and cars to the underground car park.

Left
Plans, axonometric and street elevation

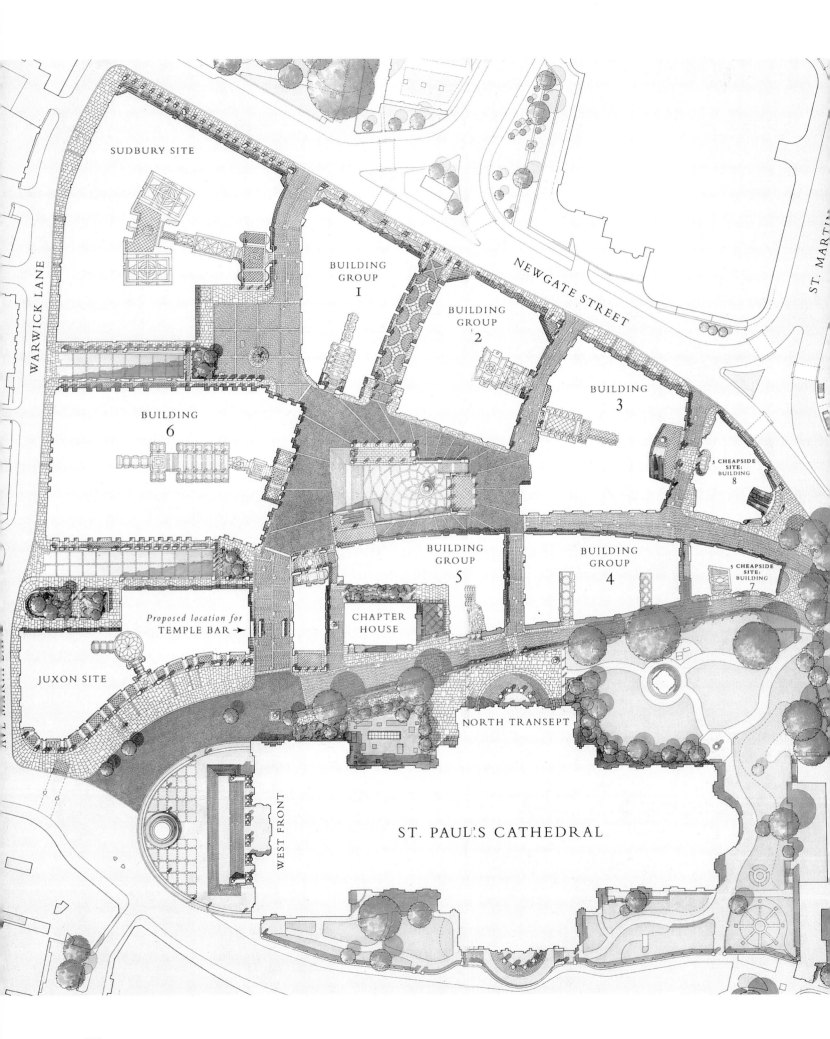

SUDBURY SITE

WARWICK LANE

BUILDING GROUP I

NEWGATE STREET

BUILDING GROUP 2

BUILDING 3

BUILDING 6

5 CHEAPSIDE SITE: BUILDING 8

Proposed location for
TEMPLE BAR →

BUILDING GROUP 5

BUILDING GROUP 4

5 CHEAPSIDE SITE: BUILDING 7

CHAPTER HOUSE

JUXON SITE

ST. MARTIN

NORTH TRANSEPT

WEST FRONT

ST. PAUL'S CATHEDRAL

PATERNOSTER SQUARE

THE CITY OF LONDON

Modern Classicism in architecture began in the early eighties and quickly became a crusade. One of the major classical urban projects in Britain involves Paternoster Square, an area whose post-war redevelopment compromised the historic relationship between St. Paul's Cathedral and the City of London, leaving a legacy of tall office buildings and windy pedestrian precincts in which all traces of the site's medieval past had been submerged.

Until it was destroyed by a bomb in the 1940s this had always been a thriving commercial area and indeed takes its name from the makers of rosary beads, or Paternosters, who lived next to the Cathedral precinct from the 13th century until the Reformation. Other commercial activities in Paternoster Row at that time were all in some way connected with the Cathedral and included stationers and text writers; by the early 16th century the area had become the centre of England's printing and publishing industries.

The new masterplan aims to restore the traditional urban grain of the area by recreating the central Square and the ground level pattern of pedestrian streets and lanes. The buildings facing the Cathedral will be aligned in such a way as to restore the perimeter of the Churchyard, and the area of landscaped gardens around the Cathedral will be enhanced.

This scheme has brought together the key figures in the classical movement in Britain, including Robert Adam, Demetri Porphyrios, John Simpson and Quinlan Terry. It has has also involved leading American Classicists Thomas H. Beeby and Allan Greenberg, two heirs to a tradition that has its own complex history.

The project emphasises the pedestrian (banished from ground level in the 1960s' scheme) and architecture on a human scale. It provides a picturesque townscape that will revive the area with much-needed shops, restaurants, entertainment facilities and open public spaces for the enjoyment of people working in the City of London and those visiting St. Paul's Cathedral.

Masterplan
Opposite
The proposed masterplan

Overleaf
The Square
(Painting by Carl Laubin.)

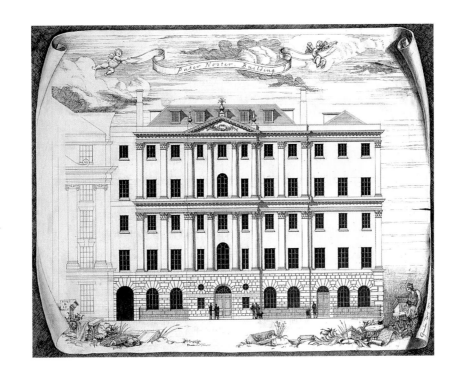

Building Group 4
Allan Greenberg Associates
USA
Opposite, top
St. Paul's Churchyard elevation

Building Group 5
John Simpson & Partners
United Kingdom
Opposite, centre
Paternoster Square elevation

Building Group 6
Hammond Beeby and Babka
USA

Opposite, bottom
Paternoster Row elevation

Building Group 7
Quinlan Terry
United Kingdom
Above, top
St Paul's Church Yard elevation

Building Group 8
Hammond Beeby and Babka
USA
Above, bottom
Cheapside elevation

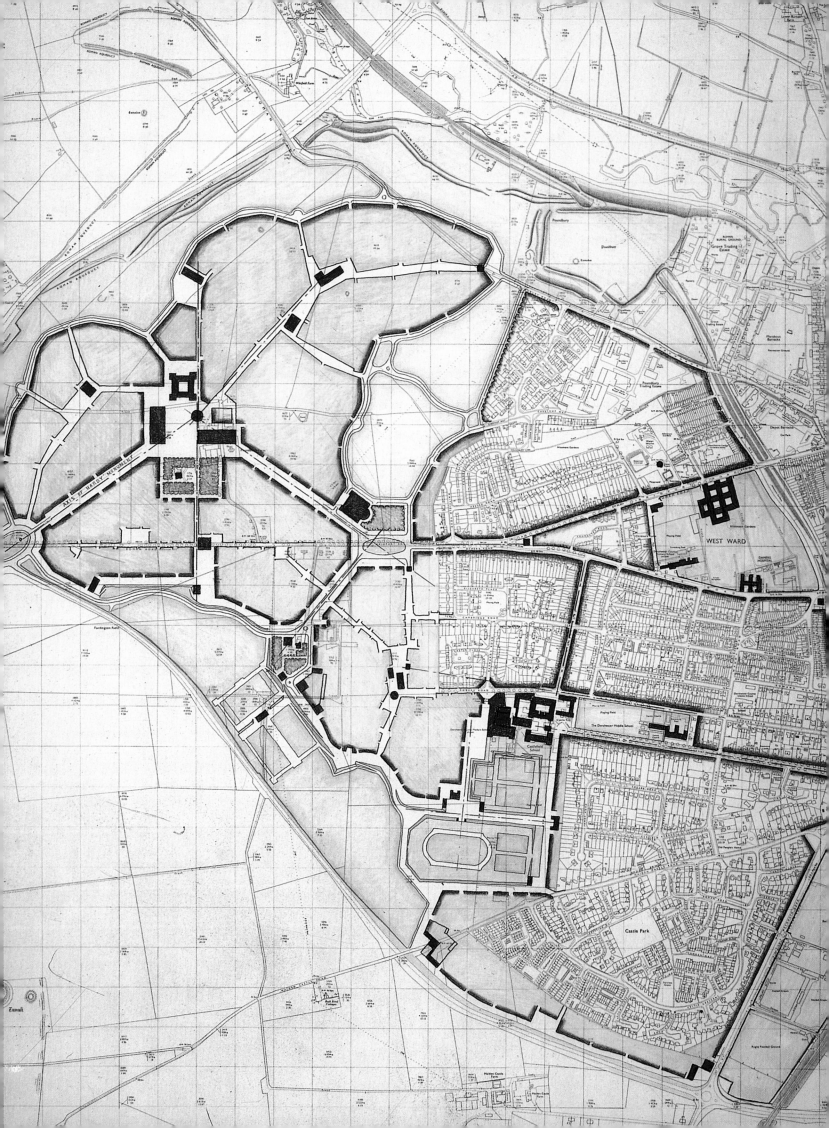

POUNDBURY

DORSET, UNITED KINGDOM

Poundbury is on the outskirts of the expanding county town of Dorchester, which did not escape the dramatic civic transformations that took place in Britain in the 1960s, assuming a largely administrative and commercial role for the suburbs proliferating around it. As has happened in similar situations throughout the country, this growth put tremendous pressure on the historic core, causing traffic congestion and destruction of the older fabric.

In 1988 Leon Krier was commissioned by the Duchy of Cornwall to consult with local authorities to find a way of reversing this trend. The Prince of Wales, with the Duchy, was determined that Poundbury would be a modern development that respected the traditions of the past while looking forward to the requirements of the twenty-first century and beyond.

Krier studied the patterns of traditional Dorset villages, their typical grouping around a common, the hierarchy of streets and the types of buildings and materials used. On the basis of his research he proposed integrating uses – rather than dividing them as has been standard planning practice since the end of World War II – and organizing future growth around several new, village-sized districts of under one hundred acres and 800 households each.

The first of these, Middle Farm, is well under way and focuses on a central square with a tower as a landmark. High streets radiate from it, reaching out to existing suburbs, an improved public park and the new Poundbury districts that occupy higher elevations around Poundbury Farm. The whole plan is defined by local topography.

Poundbury is designed to grow gradually over the next decades in response to market demand. The architecture does not represent any particular period but respects local vernacular styles. The design reflects the English village tradition, with the great variety of urban plots creating attractive streetscapes. But the philosophy of Poundbury is not just about architecture; it is about the careful, detailed planning of an attractive, modern and pleasing place in which people can live, work, shop and play.

Opposite
Site plan showing existing and new quarters
Overleaf
Bird's eye view of the development
Page 192
Plan of the Middle Farm quarter
Pages 193 à 195
Middle Farm street views

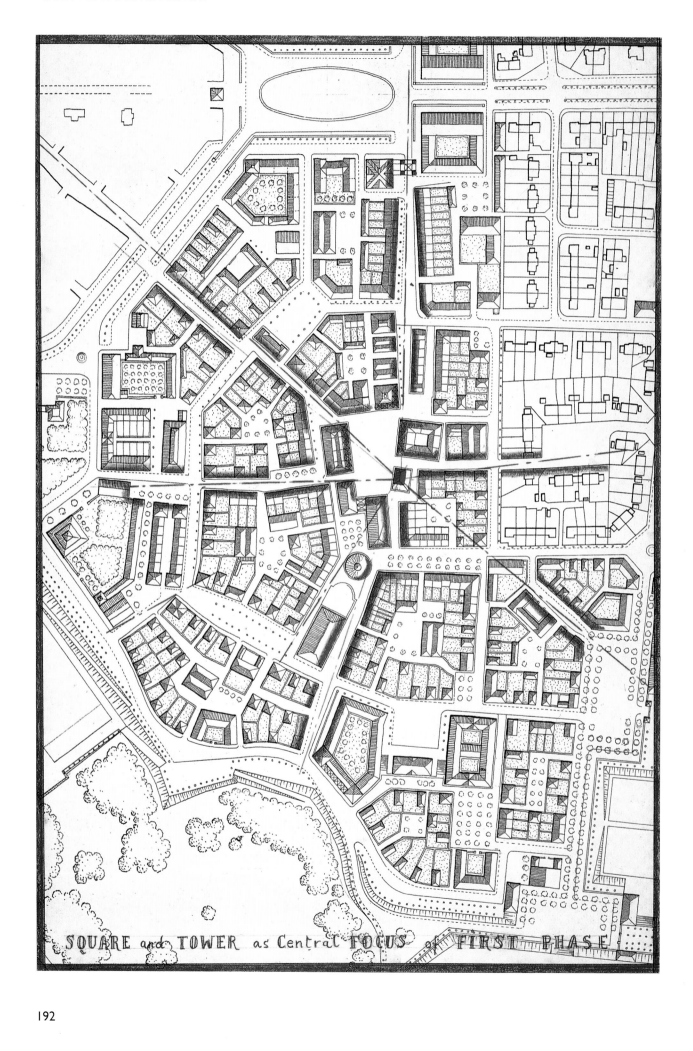

SQUARE and TOWER as Central FOCUS of FIRST PHASE

WINDSOR
FLORIDA, USA

Located on a barrier island on the east Florida coast, near the town of Vero Beach, Windsor was designed as a resort, surrounded by a golf course, polo fields and tennis courts. These leisure activities provide a green perimeter around the site, bounded by the Indian River and the Atlantic Ocean. Despite its recreational premise, Windsor was designed as a functional community.

The regulations successfully proposed by the architects codified the local vernacular. They were based on the concept of Seaside, which was nothing short of revolutionary in America; in its reconsideration of planning regulations previously considered immutable, Seaside was the architectural equivalent of throwing down the gauntlet. It has served as a prototype for what is now termed "the New Urbanism," an imperfectly understood, yet powerful image of a return to the humane, vital, and comprehensible small towns typical of the United States between the wars. The master planners of Seaside, and now of Windsor, Andreas Duany and Elizabeth Plater-Zyberk, were determined to overturn ordinances enacted after World War II, such as compartmentalized zoning and street-width requirements, that have resulted in the destruction of such towns. They advocate a return to mixed use, and a hierarchy of streets to encourage slower speeds and thus pedestrian activity. Their premise is urban places for people rather than cars, designed with planning principles that encourage human, rather than vehicular activity. The result in Windsor is a harmonious continuity throughout the village.

Because of the proximity of the Caribbean, and the similarity of these features to architecture there, many urban traditions from the islands were also adopted, giving Windsor a light and carefree aspect that balances the underlying regularity provided by the framework of the code.

This casual appearance can be deceptive, since, as Andreas Duany has said: "Traditional towns are extremely resilient and able to sustain modern life. Don't let planners tell you they don't work. What doesn't work is modern, congested suburbs."

Windsor
Florida, USA
The Urban Regulations of Windsor require that houses and continuous garden walls be built at the property line, defining the streets and squares of the village while forming private gardens. The housing is low density (300 houses on 416 acres). With the exception of the Poundbury Code, Windsor probably has the most precise small town code in existence. Streets vary in size and character from the broad entrance boulevard with its avenue of trees to small neighbourhood streets.
Opposite
Top: *Aerial view of houses designed by Scott Merrill, Clem Schaub and Armando Montero*
Bottom: *Aerial view of houses by Leslie Rebanks and Scott Merrill*

**Andres Duany and
Elizabeth Plater-Zyberk**

Coral Gables, Florida, USA

*The Architectural Regulations
provide for the vernacular architecture
of the region, with masonry first floor,
wood construction above, porches,
balconies and roof overhangs.*

Above:
*Exterior view of Dog Trot House and
Windsor I House*
Opposite
Top: *Windsor I House, view into
courtyard*
Bottom: *Dog Trot House, view
into courtyard*

Clem Schaub

USA

Preceding pages
Garden view of Sideyard House

Scott Merrill

Vero Beach, Florida, USA

Windsor was intended to be turned over to many architects once the new principles had been enacted, and Merrill Hatch's contribution, as indicated here, shows the distinctly classical direction that many of the participants took. This raises an interesting issue; the extent to which the call for a return to tradition – as clearly issued by the masterplanners – equates with this response. The answer is not easy. There was, of course, a strong Greek Revival movement in America in the late eighteenth and early nineteenth century, and Merrill Hatch's houses at Windsor clearly evoke this tradition. Their use of pure Platonic forms and proportions, squares, cubes, and rectangles divided according to the golden section, add an additional layer of difficulty to the response, giving their work a multi-faceted quality with wide appeal, and making it difficult to identify in stylistic terms.

Above
Exterior view of Windsor Rowhouses
Opposite
Exterior views of Tennis Cottages

BIOGRAPHIES

Adam, Robert
Born in 1948 in Great Britain
Graduated from Regent Street
Polytechnic, London in 1973
Won a scholarship to the British
School in Rome the same year
On his return began practice as
Winchester Design in Hampshire, now
Robert Adam Architects, Winchester
Author of *Classical Architecture: A
Complete Handbook*, *Buildings by
Design* and various papers on
architectural and urban design
SELECTED BUILDINGS & PROJECTS
Dogmersfield Park, Hampshire;
Ashmolean Humanities Centre,
Oxford University (ongoing since
1992); conversion, alteration and
extension of Rhodes House, Oxford;
village and urban design projects for
the Duchy of Cornwall; restoration and
new buildings at Heveningham Hall,
Suffolk; restoration of the British
Academy, Rome (ongoing).

Blatteau, John
Born in 1943 in the United States
Graduated in architecture from the
University of Pennsylvania in1969,
gaining an MA in 1971
Founded John Blatteau Associates in
Philadelphia in 1983
Teaches at the University of
Pennsylvania where he is doing
research into the nature of classical
form and design in architecture
Member, Board of Directors, Classical
America; President, Society of
Architectural Historians, Philadelphia
Winner of numerous awards for design
excellence
SELECTED BUILDINGS & PROJECTS
Benjamin Franklin State Dining Room,
U.S. Department of State, Washington;
Riggs Bank Headquarters building,
Bethesda office and other branches;
Glassboro State College, NJ; Center

for Theological Inquiry, Princeton, NJ;
Bayonne Hospital; Hospital of the
University of Pennsylvania.

**Castro Nunes, Alberto and António
Maria Braga**

Castro Nunes, Alberto
Born in 1952 in Portugal
Graduated from the Escola Superior de
Belas Artes, Lisbon, 1980
Founded Alberto Castro Nunes &
Antonio Maria Braga, Arquitectos, Lda
in 1990

Braga, António María
Born in 1952 in Portugal
Graduated from Escola Superior de
Belas Artes, Lisbon, 1980
Has worked with Alberto Castro Nunes
since 1980 and they have been in
practice together since 1990

Both architects write regularly in
magazines and newspapers on the
revival of the vernacular and classical
architecture in Portugal
SELECTED BUILDINGS & PROJECTS
Archaeological Museum at Odrinhas;
Fundação Ricardo Espirito Santo Silva
Arts and Crafts Museum, Lisbon;
Law Courts, Serta; Town Hall,
Odemira; Art School, Odrinhas.

Dixon, Jeremy and Edward Jones

Dixon, Jeremy
Born in 1939 in England
Graduated from the Architectural
Association School in 1963
In private practice since 1977
Designed various housing projects in
London and the cafeteria and
restaurant of the Tate Gallery.

Jones, Edward
Born in 1939 in the United Kingdom

Graduated from the Architectural
Association School in 1963
Tutor at the Royal College of Art from
1975-1982 and has been visiting
professor at Harvard, Yale, Princeton
and Rice in the USA, and in Italy
In private practice since 1977
Represented the United Kingdom at
the 1980 Venice Biennale.
Publications include *Guide to the
Architecture of London* (with
Christopher Woodward)
In 1983 he won first prize in an
international competition for
Mississauga City Hall, Canada, which
when completed won the Governor-
General's Award in 1990.
SELECTED BUILDINGS & PROJECTS
Student Housing, Robert Gordon
University, Aberdeen; Study Centre,
Darwin College, Cambridge; new
science building for the University of
Portsmouth; New Galleries for the
Henry Moore Institute, Leeds (with
BDP); Royal Opera House Covent
Garden, London (with BDP)
Won the open international
competition "A Gateway for Venice" at
the 1991 Venice Biennale.

Economakis, Richard
Born in 1961 in Egypt
Graduated from Cornell University,
USA in 1983, MA in 1985
Assistant professor, University of
Notre Dame, Indiana, USA since 1995.
Worked in the offices of Demetri
Porphyrios, John Simpson, Robert
Stern and Allan Greenberg
Member, Board of Directors, Classical
Architecture League, Washington
Books edited include *Acropolis Restor-
ation*; Editor-In-Chief, *Civitas*; member
of the editorial staff of *Archi & Colonne*
SELECTED BUILDINGS & PROJECTS
Centre for Classical Studies, Nisyros,
Greece

Greenberg, Allan

Born in 1938 in South Africa
Graduated from University of
Witwatersrand, Johannesburg, in
1961; MA from Yale, USA, in 1965
In private practice since 1972
Teaches at the Universities of Yale,
Pennsylvania and Columbia
Member, Board of Directors, Society of
Architectural Historians
Author of numerous articles and
books including *Sir Edwin Lutyens: A
Twentieth Century Architect*.
SELECTED BUILDINGS & PROJECTS
Paternoster Square Office Buildings;
Seventh-Day Adventist Church of Burr
Ridge, Illinois; Tercentenary Hall,
College of William and Mary, Virginia;
News Building, Athens, Georgia;
Simon & Schuster Executive Offices,
Rockefeller Center, New York.

Hammond Beeby and Babka

The firm was founded in 1961. The
lead designer is **Thomas H. Beeby**
who graduated from Cornell University
in 1964; M.Arch. from Yale in 1965.
Was Dean of the Yale University
School of Architecture and continues
there as Professor of Architecture.
Has taught at most major American
universities including Columbia,
Harvard, Princeton, Cornell and
UCLA.
His designs have won many prizes
including six National Honor Awards of
the American Institute of Architects.
SELECTED BUILDINGS & PROJECTS
Chicago Music and Dance Theater,
Chicago; Disney Institute, Orlando,
Florida; Oriental Institute, University of
Chicago; Fourth Presbyterian Church of
Chicago (restoration, renovation and
contextual additions); Paternoster
Square Redevelopment, London;
Harold Washington Library Centre,
Chicago.

Iñiguez, Manuel and Alberto Ustarroz

Both born in 1948 in Pamplona, Spain
Both graduated from the Escuela de
Arquitectura de Navarro in 1972
Helped found the Escuela de
Arquitectura di San Sebastián where
they both teach architectural design.
They have also taught at the schools
of architecture of Miami, Liverpool,
Marseilles, Harvard and Columbia.
In private practice together since 1972
Founded the journal *Arquitectonica* in
1991
Authors of *La lección de las Ruinas
and La construcción del Lugar*
SELECTED BUILDINGS & PROJECTS
Cordobilla-Erreleka Centre, City Hall
and Hospital Centre, Lesaka; Sarasibar
House, the Swimming Club, Petrirena
House in Pamplona; and a Health Clinic
in the old city centre there.

Krier, Leon

Born in 1946 in Luxembourg
Studied architecture at the University
of Stuttgart, Germany
Has taught at the Architectural
Association and at the Royal College of
Art in London, and at Princeton
University (1974-1977). Was Jefferson
Professor at the University of Virginia
(1982) and Davenport Professor at Yale
(1990-1991)
Collaborated with James Stirling in
London from 1968 to 1974
Now lives and works in France
Awards include the Berlin Prize for
Architecture (1987), the Jefferson
Memorial Medal (1985) and the
Chicago AIA Award (1987)
Main publications: *Cities within the
City* (1977), *Rational Architecture*
(1978), *The Completion of
Washington D.C.* (1986); *New
Classicism* (1990), *Architecture+Urban
design*

SELECTED BUILDINGS & PROJECTS
Masterplan for Poundbury, Dorset,
United Kingdom; house at Seaside,
Florida, USA; Atlantis; Consultant for
Archaeological Museum, Sintra,
Portugal.

Krier, Robert

Born in 1938 in Luxembourg
Graduated from the Technical
University of Munich in 1964
Visiting Professor at the Ecole
Polytechnique Fédérale, Lausanne,
Switzerland, at Yale University and at
the Technical University of Stockholm,
Sweden
Professor at the Technical University,
Vienna
In private practice in Vienna since 1976
Lives, works and teaches in Berlin
Author of *Urban space, Architectural
Composition, Elements of
Architecture, Zeichnungen und
Skulpturen* and numerous papers on
architectural and urban design
His drawings, projects and sculpture
have been exhibited in museums and
galleries in Europe and America
SELECTED BUILDINGS & PROJECTS
Social housing at the Ritterstrasse and
Rauchstrasse, Berlin, Germany; recon-
struction of the centre of Amiens,
France; new town for 25,000 inhabi-
tants at Marne-la-Vallée, France; new
town at Potsdam-Drewitz, Germany

Lykoudis, Michael

Born in 1954 in the USA
Graduated from Cornell University,
USA in 1978; MA from the University
of Illinois in 1983
Associate Professor and Assistant
Chair at the School of the University of
Notre Dame, Indiana, USA since 1991
Set up in private practice in 1991
Author of various papers on
architectural design and urbanism

Co-Founder and President of the Classical Architecture League, Washington, DC
SELECTED BUILDINGS & PROJECTS
Lavrio Master Plan, Greece; Blacksburg Civic Centre and Public Library, USA; New Acropolis Museum in Athens; East Hampton Airport Terminal.

Minardi, Bruno
Born in 1946 in Ravenna, Italy
Graduated from the University of Venice in 1971
Practises in Ravenna and Milan
Has taught in Venice, Urbino, Bologna and London and is currently professor of architectural design at the IUAV, Venice
President of SIACE, a cultural association that organizes seminars, conventions, exhibitions and architectural publications
His designs and projects have been exhibited in museums and galleries worldwide.
SELECTED BUILDINGS & PROJECTS
The renovation of the former Dreher factory in Venice; social housing in Cesena; the restoration of Gatteo Castle. Casa Morigi in Ravenna and Villa Trombini in Marina di Ravenna, Italy

O'Connor, Liam
Born in 1961 in the United Kingdom
Graduated from the Polytechnic of Central London (now the University of Westminster) in 1988
Was Leon Krier's assistant before setting up his own architectural practice in 1989
Has taught in Rome, was adjunct professor at the University of Notre Dame, Indiana, USA, and now teaches at the Prince of Wales's Institute of Architecture, London
Special Advisor on Architecture and

Urban Design to the Secretary of State for the Environment since 1994.
Has won two international competitions: an urban design competition for the centre of Warsaw, Poland, and one for two buildings on the rue de Laeken, Brussels, Belgium
Co-edited the *Vision of Europe* catalogue and exhibition held in Italy in 1992.
SELECTED BUILDINGS & PROJECTS
Several houses at Poundbury, Dorset; a substantial family house in Belgravia, London; three masterplan projects of various sizes in the United Kingdom including a proposal for a new settlement.

Peuker, Helmut
Born in 1953 in Germany
Studied architecture at the technical universities of Braunschweig (1975-1977) and Aachen (1977-1981), and won a one-year scholarship to study Renaissance architecture in Rome (1982-1983)
Then carried out research in Renaissance architecture for two years at the Max-Planck-Institute for the History of Art in Rome (1984-1986)
Set up his own practice in Munich, Germany, in 1988
Has participated in various exhibitions including *A Vision of Europe* in Bologna, Italy.
SELECTED BUILDINGS & PROJECTS
Conversion of the Livos administra-tion building in Emern, Germany; reconstruction of various classical houses in Germany; various banks; six new apartment blocks in Berlin-Köpenick.

Porphyrios, Demetri
Born in Greece in 1949
M.Arch. and Ph.D. degrees in the history and theory of architecture from

Princeton University, USA
Has taught at the Architectural Association, the Polytechnic of Central London and the Royal College of Art in the United Kingdom; was Jefferson Professor at the University of Virginia and Davenport Professor at Yale University in the USA
Set up his own practices in London and Athens in 1978
Publications include *Sources of Modern Eclecticism*, *On the Methodology of Architectural History*, *Building and Architecture*, *Classicism Is Not a Style* and *Classical Architecture*.
SELECTED BUILDINGS & PROJECTS
Pavilions in Highgate, London; Belvedere Village, Ascot; Rural History Centre, Reading University; Workshops and Offices at Poundbury, Dorset; Inland Revenue Offices, Nottingham; New Longwall Quadrangle, Magdalen College, Oxford; Paternoster Square Office Building, City of London; Brindleyplace, Birmingham.

Robertson, Jacquelin
Born in the USA in 1933
Graduated from Yale in 1955, MA in 1961, Rhodes Scholar, Magdalen College, Oxford, 1957
Dean and Commonwealth Professor at University of Virginia School of Architecture, 1981-1988; Bishop Professor of Architectural Design at Yale, 1980; Visiting Professor of Architecture at the Rhode Island School of Design 1979
Private practice since 1978, with Peter Eisenman in 1980, then set up Cooper, Robertson & Partners in 1988
SELECTED BUILDINGS & PROJECTS
Disney Celebration Master Plan and Town Centre, Florida; New Albany Community, Columbus, Ohio; Ohio State University, Fisher College of

Business, Columbus, Ohio;
Pennsylvania Avenue Triangle,
Washington, DC; private residences;
Weatherstone Stable and Riding Ring,
Sharon, Connecticut.

Simpson, John
Born in 1954 in the United Kingdom
Graduated from the Bartlett School of
Architecture and Planning, University
of London, in 1978
Teaches at Prince of Wales's Institute
of Architecture
Set up in private practice in 1980
SELECTED BUILDINGS & PROJECTS
Masterplan for Paternoster Square,
London; Masterplan for Coldharbour
Farm, Aylesbury, Buckinghamshire,
UK; new office building at 21 Lime
Street, London; new public rooms and
restoration of Grade I Listed Buildings
at Gonville and Caius College,
Cambridge, UK.

Smith, Thomas Gordon
Born in 1948 in the USA
Graduated from the University of
California at Berkeley, gaining an MA in
1975.
Won the Rome Prize in 1979-1980 and
exhibited at the 1980 Venice Biennale
"The Presence of the Past"
Chair of the School of Architecture at
the University of Notre Dame, Indiana.
His book *Classical Architecture: Rule
and Invention* was published in 1986.
SELECTED BUILDINGS & PROJECTS
Vitruvian House, Indiana, USA; Kulb
House, Central Illinois, USA; Civic
Centre for Cathedral City, California,
USA

Spoerry, François
Born in France in 1912
Began his studies at the Ecole des
Beaux-Arts, Strasbourg; graduated
from the Ecole des Beaux-Arts,

Marseilles, in 1942
Set up his practice in Mulhouse in
1945
Author of *A Gentle Architecture*,1989
SELECTED BUILDINGS & PROJECTS
Port Grimaud, Var, France; Gassin, Var,
France; town centre, Plessis-Robinson,
Paris; Port Liberté, NY, USA.

Tagliaventi & Associates

Tagliaventi, Ivo
Born in 1923 in Italy
Graduated from the Institute of
Architecture and Urbanism in Bologna.
Assistant professor and later professor
and director of the Institute of
Architecture and Urbanism, University
of Bologna
Went into practice with Giovanni
Michelucci in 1979
Author of *Idee per la città*, *L'organismo
architettonico* and of several essays
and books on Gothic Architecture and
Viollet-le-Duc.
Member, Town Planning Committee of
the Municipality of Florence; President
of *A Vision of Europe* Committee;
director of *A&C International*
architecture magazine
SELECTED BUILDINGS & PROJECTS
Architect of Volkswagen Italy, designed
their headquarters and warehouses in
Bologna and Verona; designed the new
Stadium and Sports facilities in
Messina and collaborated with James
Stirling on the new urban centre for
Bologna-Casalecchio.

Tagliaventi, Gabriele
Born in 1960 in Italy
Graduated from the Institute of
Architecture and Urbanism, University
of Bologna, in 1985
Assistant professor of Town Planning
at the University of Bologna and
Professor of Architectural Projects at

the University of Parma.
Has won prizes in several international
competitions including the
Reconstruction of the Rue de Laeken
in Brussels and the Reconstruction of
Warsaw City Core; and the New
College of South Stockholm.
Author of *Garden Cities*, and *Urban
Renaissance*. Deputy Director of *A&C
International* architecture magazine
Joint curator of *A Vision of Europe*
exhibition in Bologna (1992) and *Urban
Renaissance* (1996)
SELECTED BUILDINGS & PROJECTS
Two residential buildings in the Rue de
Laeken in the centre of Brussels; a
villa in the Appennines; reconstruction
and extension of a building in Bologna;
masterplan, with Ivo Tagliaventi, of a
new urban district in Pieve di Cento.

Terry, Quinlan
Born in 1937 in the United Kingdom
Graduated from the Architectural
Association, London, in 1961
Joined Raymond Erith and worked
with him until his death in 1973. Then
continued the practice alone.
SELECTED BUILDINGS & PROJECTS
Richmond Riverside; the Ionic, Veneto
and Gothick Villas in Regent's Park,
London, for the Crown Estate
Commissioners; New Lecture Theatre,
Junior Common Room, Maitland
Robinson Library and a new residential
building for Downing College, Cam-
bridge; New Brentwood Cathedral;
Gloucester Magistrates Courthouse;
three State Drawing Rooms at 10
Downing Street, London.

PHOTOCREDITS

Pages 2, 24, 25, 50, 52, 55, 62, 63, 64-65 Tim Buchman
Pages 10, 11, 29, 144, 146, 148-9, 153, 154, 155, 157, 158, 159 bottom Nick Carter
Page 13 Kim Zwarts
Page 23 F. Achlou
Page 26, 137, 138, 141 Atelier F. Spoerry
Page 30 Joe Low
Pages 36, 53, 54, 56, 57, 58, 59, 60-61 Richard Cheek
Pages 66-69 Jon Miller, Hedrich-Blessing
Pages 79 top, 80-81 Robert Grahn
Pages 84, 86-89 Marco Buzzoni
Pages 92, 94, 95, 180 Liam O'Connor
Pages136, 139, 140 Claude Gaspari
Pages 142, 174, 175 Industrialfoto, Bologna
Page 151 Les Canham
Pages 158 bottom, 159 top Crown Estate
Pages 174, 179, 180 S. Desauw
Pages 193-195 Andreas Papadakis
Page196 Dick Dickinson
Pages 198, 199, 200-201, 202 Th. Delbeck Photography
Page 203 Wm C. Minarich

All photographs not credited were provided by the architects featured and reproduced
with their permission.

ACKNOWLEDGEMENTS

I should like to thank my publisher, Jean-François Gonthier and his staff for their encouragement and support; James Steele for his research and contributions generally as well as the introductory essay; the photographers who have generously provided the illustrations; the chief designer, Constantine Milides, and my assistant Lotte Elkiaer. Finally, I should like to express my great appreciation to all the architects whose work is presented here, and especially to Leon Krier, Allan Greenberg and Jaquelin Robertson for their advice and suggestions during numerous discussions.

I am also grateful to the author and the publishers for permission to reproduce the extract on pages 162-171 from: *Architecture Choix ou Fatalité* by Leon Krier, published in 1996 in French by the Institut Français d'Architecture and Norma, Paris and in English by Andreas Papadakis Publisher.

Andreas Papadakis.

Printed in Italy
by OFFSET PRINT VENETA
Verona